daughters gone WILD

dads gone CRAZY

*Battle-Tested Tips from a
Father and Daughter
Who survived the Teen Years*

CHARLES STONE AND HEATHER STONE

W PUBLISHING GROUP™

www.wpublishinggroup.com

A Division of Thomas Nelson, Inc.
www.ThomasNelson.com

Unless otherwise noted, Scripture references are from The Holy Bible, New International Version (NIV). Copyright © 1973, 1978, 1984, International Bible Society. Used by permission of Zondervan Bible Publishers.

Other Scripture references are from the following sources:

> The Message (MSG), copyright © 1993. Used by permission of NavPress Publishing Group.

> New American Standard Bible (NASB), © 1960, 1977 by the Lockman Foundation.

> The Contemporary English Version (CEV) © 1991 by the American Bible Society. Used by permission.

> The Holy Bible, New Living Translation (NLT) (Wheaton, Ill.: Tyndale House Publishers, 1996). Used by permission.

Interior design by Inside Out Design & Typesetting,
Fort Worth, Texas

Library of Congress Cataloging-in-Publication Data
Stone, Charles, 1954–
 Daughters gone wild—dads gone crazy : battle-tested tips from a father and daughter who survived the teen years / Charles Stone and Heather Stone.
  p. cm.
Summary: "Firsthand experience between a father and a rebellious daughter, and the steps they took to make the relationship better."—Provided by publisher.
Includes bibliographical references.
ISBN 0-8499-0434-X (trade paper)
1. Parenting—Religious aspects—Christianity. 2. Parent and teenager—Religious aspects—Christianity. 3. Fathers and daughters—Religious aspects—Christianity. 4. Child rearing—Religious aspects—Christianity.
5. Stone, Charles, 1954–6.
Stone, Heather, 1982–   I. Stone, Heather 1982—   II. Title.
BV4529.S86   2005
248.8'45—dc22   2005000781

Printed in the United States of America
05 06 07 RRD 9 8 7 6 5 4 3

CONTENTS

Contents

Acknowledgments

Charles Stone

Before I acknowledge those who made this book possible, I must thank my wife, Sherryl. Not only did she write each "Mom-to-Mom" section, but her heart is imprinted into each word. For she, too, shared this journey with Heather and me.

My list of thanks for where I am in life would fill many pages. So I've limited my thanks to those who've impacted my writing ministry. To Jan Johnson, who, at a writer's conference taught this pre-novice to begin my writing career with articles. Thanks, Jan, for the sage advice. To Kristi Rector, who actually liked the first magazine article I ever wrote. Thanks, Kristi, for publishing it in *Rev. Magazine*. To the Mount Hermon Christian Writer's Conference for teaching me how to write. Thanks, teachers and fellow writers, for sharing your craft with me. To Dave Talbot, who coordinates the Mount Hermon conference each year. Thanks, Dave, for interviewing Heather and me during the conference—God used those three minutes to throw open the door of opportunity. To Steve Laube, our original agent who landed our contract. Thanks, Steve, for believing in us. To my writer's group in Modesto, California. Thanks, guys, for your friendship, critiques, and encouragement you gave me each time we met. To Greg Daniel, our editor at W Publishing Group. Thanks, Greg, for the gentle way you helped us improve the manuscript. To a kind, older woman who sat at my lunch table during a writer's conference in 2002. I don't even know your name, but that day you "told" me that I should write the book with Heather. Thanks, ma'am, for the challenge. I never forgot it. One day on the other side I'll look you up to personally say, "Thanks." God placed you in my life that day "for such a time as this."

Heather Stone

I want to say thank you . . . thank you to all of the "earth-bound angels" who perhaps unknowingly touched my life and left an indelible mark on my soul; who taught me how to feel, how to express myself, how to love, and how to be fully alive. To Mrs. Dietz, for saving my life with your 2 a.m. prayers. I fully believe I wouldn't be here if it weren't for you. To Jo, for being the beautiful person you are and for touching my very soul. "Words are never enough." To Misty (mantis), and that night with the puzzle, for forgiveness, patience, for changing my life, and so much more. To Heather, my "firecracker" who is always, always there for me. To Nick, my oftentimes rock, for your unwavering strength, support, and gentleness. You make me feel safe. To Jackson, though you probably can't even understand what I'm writing, I don't think I've ever met anyone else who basks in the presence of God as you do. To Mrs. Kullman, for all your letters and prayers though we barely know each other. To all those at Joshua Wilderness Institute, Darin, the Bradens, Mr. Phillips, Norm, and everyone else: thank you for making my life something so much more than I ever imagined. To Paps, for hugs, love, and always believing I would turn around. To Karen, for your unconditional love and faithful prayers. To Granny and Papa, for your love, warmth, and prayers. To everyone else in my family, thank you. To Josh, for being a strong Christian man I can look up to. To Tiffany, for her strength, diligence, and pure heart. To Mom and Dad: in case one day goes by that I forget to say this—I love you, I love you, I love you. I wouldn't be the person I am today without each and every one of you. And to those I haven't mentioned, you know who you are, I love you all and can't wait to be with you for eternity. To God be the glory forever and ever.

introduction

How to Get the Most Out of this Book

The most rewarding relationship a man can have,
beyond his relationship with his wife,
is with his daughter.
—Charles Stone

For Dads

A handful of fidgety people sat in the nearly empty room. We took our seats at the back, and after a few moments the bailiff barked his customary, "All rise!" A dark-haired judge emerged from the side door. He seemed to float to his bench in his ankle-length black robe. I could feel my shoulders begin to tighten as we nervously sat in courtroom A.

"Charles and Sherryl Stone vs. Heather Stone: Case number 43. Please come forward," he bellowed.

The bailiff opened the waist-high swinging door that led to the judge's bench. The judge motioned for us to sit at the well-worn Formica covered table in front of him. He peered over his black-rimmed glasses. "So, what's the problem?" he asked.

With a dry mouth I muttered, "We just can't handle our oldest daughter anymore. She runs away, stays out all night with boys, uses drugs and alcohol, curses us, and skips school. We've consulted a half-dozen psychologists. We've pled with her, fought with her, and grounded her. We're desperate. We need your help."

He glared at her for what seemed like a full minute, glanced down at his notes, looked up, and began his stern discourse. "Young lady, this is serious. I'm placing you under house arrest and assigning you a probation officer. You *will* meet with her weekly. You *will* take a weekly drug test. You *will* obey your parents. You will *not* run away again. Should you attempt to, the monitor we will place around your ankle *will* alert us. And we *will* find you."

With a menacing tone he added, "Don't let me see you in here again!" The crack of his gavel echoed in the courtroom as he slammed it onto his desk and said, "Next case."

This true experience epitomized our six-year battle during the stormy teen years of my oldest daughter, Heather's. Once a compliant, top-of-her-class, prim and proper daughter, within just a few months after her thirteenth birthday she morphed into a drug-using, sexually active, angry, in-your-face teenaged scofflaw. Navigating her through those years almost drowned us in a vortex of pain, anger, and disappointment. At times we felt we could barely gasp for air between each new conflict. Were it not for a few relational "life preservers" that we clung to, our relationship with Heather could not have weathered those tumultuous years from age thirteen to eighteen.

When Heather entered her teenage years, my wife and I were prepared to apply all the sound parenting techniques we had read in parenting books. We quoted Bible verses about morality, children, and the spiritual life. We taught often on the importance of obeying parents. We made her attend church and youth group activities twice a week. We sent her to Christian schools. We seldom missed our family nights because we believed the experts who wrote that Christian families bond through quality family time.

Every Tuesday night, my wife, Sherryl, and I loaded our three kids in our sand-colored Dodge Caravan and drove to the mall to "bond." We strolled into the food court and each of us chose our favorite meal. Even before we had picked up our orders, our problems began. Heather, dressed in her grungiest clothes, combat boots, and bootblack eye shadow, began her theatrics. When we asked her to do something, she mustered up a made-for-Hollywood performance of "let's see how miserable I can make my parents" with her sighs and "whatever's" as she rolled her eyes. Family nights ended up revolving around her. Eventually, she sat at a table by herself. If we were lucky, she sat within twenty feet of our table. So much for bonding.

We also tried to harness Heather with contracts—written lists of behaviors we expected from her. I like lists so much that I even make lists for my lists. I assumed Heather would like them too. I believed that once she followed a few lists, she would experience "conversion by list" and become her old sweet, compliant self again.

I designed several contracts with lists . . . year after year. All came with a place for name, date, and two signatures. She signed her line. I signed mine. I created my favorite one with a computer spreadsheet program complete with expectations, due dates, privileges, and status bars. (This helped me feel I got my money's worth from my engineering degree.) Others included check boxes or bullet points. There were a few times of desperation when I added exclamation points after key expectations, hoping to "guilt" her into obedience. I tried to communicate, *Heather, you'd better obey or your dad will die of a massive coronary and you will be very, very sad!* Dumb idea. Guilt didn't work. I learned to better cope and parent more constructively.

I taped these contract-lists on her bedroom door and her bathroom mirror. I wallpapered the refrigerator door with them. I

Mom's Tip

Mom, to help ease the tension between your daughter and her dad, carve out some time just for you and your daughter. Go shopping or see a chick-flick together.

stuck them on the cabinet shelves where we kept the Fritos and Chips Ahoy. I laid a trail of them in the hall that led into her room. I set them on her bed. I crammed them in her bologna sandwiches. (Not really, but I considered it.)

Although these techniques worked well with my two other children, did they work for Heather? Nope. Not after she turned thirteen. Instead, our experience with Heather gave us . . .

- Twenty different psychologists, counselors, and psychiatrists who tried to help her.
- Seven stays in four different programs for troubled teens.
- A sheriff's escort to one treatment center.
- Drugs, alcohol, and destructive relationships with boys.
- Twelve middle and high schools (four kicked her out).
- A court-mandated house arrest, complete with a homing device around her ankle that would alert the authorities if she ran away.
- Weekly visits to her probation officer.
- Three 911 calls to the police because we feared she would hurt herself or us.
- Endless arguments, conflict, and verbal fights..

Dads, if contracts, lists, family nights, Bible lectures, and church youth groups work for you, perhaps you don't need this book. If they don't, you've picked the right resource to find help and hope. After those tough years, God did restore my relationship with Heather. Although I'm sure those techniques we originally tried did influence her eventual return, the relational life preservers we include in this book made the biggest difference.

These battle-tested tips didn't magically appear. I learned them through trial and error—many errors. And only in retrospect have I been able to crystallize them. Had I known how profoundly these choices would impact our relationship, I would have more deliberately used them.

Introduction

This book differs from most other fathering books in several ways. Some authors give advice gained through their experiences with other parents and teens but not through firsthand experience. Other books offer help only from a dad's perspective and not from a daughter's.

This book, however, combines the firsthand perspectives of both a father and a daughter. Heather and I want to share with you the nine relational life preservers we gleaned from our crucible of pain. These kept our relationship alive, though sometimes by only a thread. The lessons arose not only out of our successes but our many failures too. While we focus on the father-daughter relationship, moms and sons will find these "life preservers" helpful as well.

These simple principles can help bridge the relational void you and your daughter feel. We don't espouse a simple recipe for success, nor easy 1-2-3 steps that guarantee instant results. We're convinced, though, that these proven life preservers can help you sustain a positive relationship while you ride out the storm. Like a boat's life preservers, they don't get you out of the storm. Instead, they provide something to cling to so that you keep your head above the water when waves of anger, disappointment, and hopelessness crash over you.

In the next nine chapters you'll journey with Heather and me as we share our story and apply biblical truth to these nine relational life preservers.

1. Respond to the early warning signs; don't panic!
2. Resist the urge to turn words into weapons.
3. Make the tough calls when you must.
4. Stoke the relationship fire to keep love alive.
5. Reconnect through gifts from the heart.
6. Laugh between the tears.
7. Choose your battles wisely . . . and lose some on purpose.
8. Cling to hope when you're at the bottom.
9. Soften the reentry as much as possible.

We've organized this book to make it easy for you and your daughter to read and apply its suggestions. I wrote the chapter sections geared toward dads, and Heather wrote the chapter sections targeted for daughters. Your daughter can go directly to her sections by finding the "For Daughters" page numbers in the Contents. You will get the greatest benefit if you both read the book and try the Relationship Lifters at the end of each section. So, you might want to purchase a book for each of you. We've also included a "For Dads' Eyes Only" chapter about parental guilt and a "For Daughters' Eyes Only" chapter about the consequences of premarital sex.

> ### Mom's Tip
>
> Mom, suggest ways to encourage your daughter to read the book as well. She might listen to you more readily than to Dad. But first talk with her father to determine the best action plan.

Do whatever it takes to motivate your daughter to read the sections written for her, but don't try to force her. My best advice: *bribe her!* Extend her curfew one hour each time she reads a chapter. Let her talk on the phone for an extra hour. Offer to pay her five bucks for every chapter she reads. Go away for a weekend and tell her she can have a party at your house while you're gone. Just kidding.

Consider a conversation something like this: "Honey, I know you and I aren't doing well in our relationship. I want to change, and I'm reading this book written by a dad and his twenty-two-year-old daughter who really messed her life up. She and her dad now have a great relationship, and this book tells what they learned that kept their relationship from totally falling apart. The daughter wrote a section in each chapter just for teen girls who struggle with their dads. I was wondering if you'd consider reading those sections. I'd be willing to make it worth your while with [your incentive]."

Heather and I believe that you can brave the storm and come out stronger on the other end. We pray that God will use this book to rekindle a new love between you and your daugh-ter. May one day you experience what Luke described happened between the prodigal son and his father in their renewed relationship: "And they began to have a wonderful time" (Luke 15:24, MSG).

Heather and I know the beauty of a restored relationship. You and your daughter can experience that same joy.

A WORD TO MOMS

My wife, Sherryl, and I formed a united team to deal with Heather's difficulties. She stood with me at every turn and provided just as much direction for Heather as I did. Because of the unique nature of the father-daughter bond, however, I speak directly to dads. Since a difficult dad-daughter relationship also affects mothers, I've designed each chapter with mothers in mind as well. The principles don't apply only to dads, but also to moms. At the end of each chapter you'll find a special section, *Mom to Mom*, written from my wife's perspective. She shares from the heart of one mom to another. Also, you'll occasionally find a Mom's Tip sidebar, offering a parenting suggestion just for you.

For Daughters

"I never wanted to live in this prison anyway!" I screamed down the hall.

The bookbag on my shoulder was crammed with clothes, makeup, and my mother's jewelry, which I had stolen and planned to pawn. I pounded down the hall to the back door. Outside, my friend honked his car horn. Hand on the doorknob, I turned, looked my father square in the face with hatred, and said slowly, "I don't need you. I never have. And I never will."

I turned my back to him, slammed the door as forcefully as I could, and was gone.

I never imagined that the man I treated this way would one day be my role model, my confidant, and my friend—in short, the most important man in my life.

Who would have thought the fights would be replaced with "date nights," repulsion would turn into respect, and hatred would turn into love?

It didn't start out bad. When I was younger, I epitomized the stereotypical "perfect" pastor's daughter: earner of straight As, neighborhood baby-sitter, a class president at my Christian school. However, my peers basically ignored and often shunned me. I had few friends. I wasn't "cool" and didn't fit in. Kids never invited me to hang out with them, and I always felt inferior.

Perhaps I was fed up with being made fun of, or I finally wanted to be "cool." Maybe it was just curiosity. One thing happened for sure: when I hit thirteen, everything changed.

Sadly, my story isn't all that unique. I know many girls who are just as I was—into drugs, sex, alcohol; in and out of treatment centers for delinquents; and at war with their parents.

I morphed from perfect goody-goody to bat-out-of-hell *wild* and stayed that way for many years. In spite of twelve different schools (four of which expelled me), more than fifteen psychiatrists and psychologists, numerous rehabs, years on probation, and house arrest twice, I hardly changed. It started with smoking cigarettes in my room. (Don't try it—the smell makes it obvious, even with the windows open!) and expulsion from my Christian school. On to the drinking, the drugs, the boys, the sneaking out, and the beginning of many stays in programs for "troubled" teens—that became my life.

School? If I even attended, I couldn't stay awake because I'd been out all night. If I showed up, I usually skipped out by lunchtime. I began to fail classes.

Introduction

Church? God? They were both only a distant memory and an object of my disgust. I didn't want to hear some religious quick-fix answer for what I was going through. It finally took a literal near-death experience to open my eyes to what I was doing to myself, my life, and my parents. It took a "God experience" to change things truly for the better.

Though I thought I was having the time of my life, my journal indicates something different:

> My body just keeps going on and existing kind of like I'm just left behind... I just need a purpose... I am so unhappy. But it's not like genuine hurt, stinging, aching hurt. It's a numbness... I feel as cold and limp and dead as the icicles hanging from the trees outside. ... I feel so much as though I'm on the outside looking in. ...

I find one journal entry after another that chronicles bitter anger at my father. As I reflect on those turbulent years, however, I see things in a completely different light. My dad defended me to principals, counselors, and my probation officer. He was a constant in my life, no matter how many problems I caused, no matter how many rehabs I went through, and no matter how many times I failed. My friends all went their separate ways. The drugs wore off, the boys left, and the alcohol almost killed me. Who never stopped loving me unconditionally? God and my dad.

You may feel that your dad is so crazy he should be committed to the nearest mental ward. He may act weird. (My dad has fake rotting teeth he wears to play jokes on people.) He may dress strangely. (My dad's favorite "accessories" include his red-checkered fanny pack and his double-brimmed fishing hat.) He may irritate you, try to control you, and at times, seem unbearable. But one thing I learned: his behavior is not *designed* to irritate you. I can promise you that he loves you more than you know. Although I despised my father, disrespected him, and shunned him for years, I finally realized that he was the one who came through for me in my times of need. When no one else was around, I could always count on Dad to be there.

If you're the daughter "gone wild," I've been where you are now. My past includes not only difficult times with my father, but the consequences that I still live with today. I vowed that I would have no regrets about my past as long as I could use my experiences to help someone else. My greatest hope is that you can learn from my life and avoid many of the mistakes I made.

I'm not going to preach to you, and I'm not going to give you unrealistic suggestions. I want to help you realize that growing up doesn't have to be a constant dad-versus-daughter battle. If you only give him a chance, you will discover that he can be one of your greatest allies.

We wrote our book with separate sections for fathers and daughters. My dad writes the section for your father, and I write the section for you. At the end of each section, we will include a few items we've called Relationship Lifters. These are simple, practical ideas for bettering your relationship with your dad. They're things that worked for my dad and me when we were going through our hard times, and I hope they will work for you.

Perhaps you've found the book first, and you want to convince your dad to read it. Offer to take him on a "date" or to clean your room if he'll read some of the chapters with you. (My dad will do anything to get me to clean my room!) It might take a little convincing on your part, but I'm sure it will be worth it.

You know, things will never be perfect. Dad will always be . . . well, a dad . . . and you will always be you. The two of you will always have your differences, and this book will not turn your relationship into a fairy tale. However, with a little give-and-take, you can rediscover the relationship you were meant to have with the hero in your life you've been overlooking—your dad.

one

THE FIRST TATTOO

The wildest colts make the best horses.
—Plutarch

For Dads

Our journey didn't really begin with Heather's first tattoo at age thirteen, but about twelve years earlier.

Before Heather was born, I became a true believer in seatbelt safety. I still remember the 1960s public service seat-belt commercials and their catchy march-time jingle that encouraged drivers to buckle up. That message stuck with me and I became a seat-belt-use drill sergeant for every passenger in our car, including our children.

In the eighties, car seats were contraptions of shiny tubular bars and flimsy plastic upholstery; even without the kid they weighed as much as a John Deere forty-two-inch riding lawn mower with both grass bags full. I would not move the car even out of the driveway unless I strapped Heather into her seat. I never budged—no exceptions. Not even on one infamous day—the day I learned the meaning of the phrase "the strong-willed child."

After Heather turned one, we planned a trip to see my wife's family in Mississippi. At the time we lived in Texas and decided to fly instead of enduring the sixteen-hour drive with a one-year-old. We recruited some friends at church to ride with us to the Dallas–Fort Worth airport and then drive our car home. I lugged our heavy-as-a-John Deere-mower car seat to the backseat of our two-door Grand Prix, strapped it in, and buckled up Heather. No problem so far.

We then picked up our friends. They sat in the backseat next to Heather. Ten minutes into our drive, Heather began to utter a guttural sound as if she'd been constipated for days and was about to . . . well, you know. But that wasn't the problem. Those grunts crescendoed into earsplitting 150-decibel shrieks, equivalent to how that John Deere mower would sound with no muffler, two inches away from your ear.

A simple translation of her shrieks (we were experts in discerning Heather's unintelligible demands) might read like this: *Father, I did not want you to put me in this cheap car seat in the first place. I don't like being confined, and I want the freedom to roam in the car at my leisure. I will do as I please. So, until you take me out of this seat, I will continue to blow your eardrums out. And with a set of lungs like these, I will win.*

As a seat-belt-safety-conscious father, I pulled into the emergency lane and stopped. I got out, pulled the back of my seat forward, and leaned into Heather's face to make eye contact with her. She listened intently to my lecture on the importance of car safety and why I would not let her out of the seat. Even though my wife pleaded with me to take her out, I was her father and I knew best. I told Heather not to cry anymore and that we would continue our trip to the airport.

I sat back down, closed the door, and merged back into traffic, quite proud of my fathering skills. After approximately 6.2 seconds Heather let out another piercing howl. For the next full forty minutes we endured a non-stop concert of high-pitched grunts, growls, and howls that resulted in migraines for all. (Funny thing— our friends never again volunteered to take us to the airport. With

20/20 hindsight, I now realize they were probably as uncomfortable with my attempt to correct her as they were with her howls.

About that time, I read James Dobson's book, *The Strong-Willed Child*. Heather fit his description of a defiant child. The book's principles worked okay with Heather for the first thirteen years. That is, until that first tattoo.

Heather attended a Christian school through the eighth grade and always performed at the top of her class. She impressed her teachers with her grades, her positive attitude, and her in-telligence. Then toward the end of the eighth grade, we began to discover that the child-rearing principles that had worked up to that time quit working. We began to argue more, and she began to defy us. We felt confident, however, that she'd soon grow out of that stage. Summer vacation would certainly bring back the compliant Heather we knew, we thought. (A sure sign of clueless parents.)

The school held a graduation ceremony for the eighth-grade students on their last day. As my wife and I drove to the school, I thought about Heather's accomplishments and her future high school years. I proudly mused, *My firstborn is growing up.*

We pulled into the gravel parking lot. As we headed for the gym, we sensed a buzz among the kids. We took seats about halfway back. About fifteen minutes later, the ceremony began. As the students marched in to the tune of "Pomp and Circumstance" and sat down, we spotted Heather. I noticed she wore a very short dress I had never seen before, and

Mom's Tip

Mom, you'll probably see your daughter's strong-willed nature before your husband sees it. Try to help him understand what may lie on the horizon. Don't nag, but persist until he begins to recognize the nature she was born with and the need to respond to it properly.

I felt uncomfortable about it. Usually she wore very conservative clothes.

The principal greeted everyone, prayed, and gave a short speech about the past year. He challenged the students to do their best as they moved into high school. As he called each student's name, he or she walked to the podium to receive a graduation certificate. Because of the small class size, it didn't take long for him to get to Heather. I swelled with pride.

As she reached out to receive her diploma, I noticed a disapproving look on the principal's face. I couldn't imagine why until she turned around to walk back to her seat. Her eyes locked with mine. She glared at me, and the defiance in her eyes seemed to say, *Dad, I'm throwing down the gauntlet. You'd better buckle up because now things are going to be different. I'm all grown up. You can't tell me what to do anymore.*

At that moment I saw what had shocked the principal. When she had filed in, only her left side was visible. When I saw her right side, there, on her right upper arm, in royal blue, crimson, and white, oozing with bravado, blazed a *Superman tattoo.*

I think the *S* on the tattoo morphed into a wicked grin. My daughter, a preacher's kid, had gotten a tattoo without permission. My blood pressure sky-rocketed. My face flushed red with anger. I felt a hundred disapproving stares from other parents. They, too, saw this act of willful defiance that signaled the beginning of World War III. This meant spiritual warfare.

I would now have to nip in the bud this defiance before it escalated into something like, well, body piercing. I laugh now, since a few years later Heather came home with her tongue pierced. My response then, after I had learned not to panic, was a muted, "Yuk, Heather. That must have hurt."

However, in that first skirmish, I ranted and fumed on the drive home about the horrors of body mutilation. I gave her this ultimatum: "You will not blatantly throw away all our Christian values by mutilating your body with a tattoo!"

4

To my chagrin, she informed me that it was a stick-on tattoo. I then got very quiet and thought, *Way to go, Charles. Was that stupid or what?*

❖——❖

The tattoo incident, although not a big deal in itself, marked her transition into adolescence and our transition into five years of relational turbulence. Had I been more prepared with a book like this one, our experience wouldn't have felt like an emotional death valley. In those early days of the storm, I panicked too often. Our other two kids, a younger brother and sister, responded to standard child-rearing and discipline techniques. But not Heather.

Even in my ignorance, though, I made a few good choices early on. I chose to stay intimately involved in my daughter's life, though I could have disengaged my heart through over-control or emotional distance. Fortunately, I didn't make all the panic-induced mistakes that could have driven a stake into the heart of our relationship.

We've collected the following battle-tested tips to help you avoid panic when your daughter shocks you with her choices. Check these out for some encouragement.

How to Apply
Relational Life Preserver 1

1. Understand that your influence matters more than you think.

During our five-year struggle, I often felt that what I said or decisions I made no difference in Heather's choices. Only in retrospect did I realize that what I believed and how I acted mattered greatly to her.

Studies bear this out. A study of twenty-two thousand children

5

found that adolescent girls aged twelve to seventeen living in families without a live-in father were almost 50 percent more likely to use illegal drugs, alcohol, or tobacco than girls living with both biological parents.[1] Another study revealed that emotionally available dads do impact their daughters' spiritual commitment.[2] Although Heather expressed little interest in developing her faith during her rebellious years, I know my emotional presence contributed to her eventual return to her spiritual roots.

Your direct involvement in your daughter's life does make a difference. We matter more than we think. Stay emotionally connected to her (see chapters 4 and 5 for ideas how). Defuse the temptation to withdraw when things get tough.

2. Admit to yourself that tough times may be in store.

After a few frustrating grocery store experiences, I now do a "buggy check" each time I pick a shopping cart. Why? It's hard to steer some buggies straight because of one misaligned wheel. Kids remind me of buggies. Many easily stay on course without much parental pressure. However, others, like Heather, require Herculean efforts to keep them even in a semi-straight line.

Adolescence complicates the life of every girl. Friendship issues, struggles with self-concept, and hormonal changes all converge at once. Their moodiness can make us feel as if a chameleon lives with us—pleasant one moment and like a deranged cat the next. Their changing bodies contribute to this emotional roller coaster.

Neuroscientists discovered that the part of the brain that helps us make sound judgments doesn't fully develop until our early twenties. Meanwhile, the part of the brain that generates raw emotion (such as anger) enters a stage of hyper-development in the teen years. This explains in part how our daughters can be so moody and make unwise decisions based on emotions alone.[3]

I had no clue about this biological change occurring in Heather. In fact, I had developed a smug attitude toward other parents with difficult teens. I identified with some people who thought that all we had to do was follow Christian principles and everything would turn out right. I discovered how naïve I was. Up to that point I had read the Bible through rose-colored glasses. I wrongly interpreted Proverbs 22:6 ("Train a child in the way he should go, and when he is old he will not turn from it"). I had believed it guaranteed parenting success as long as I followed biblical principles. Not until later did I realize that Solomon wrote the book of Proverbs as a general observation about life, not as a book of ironclad guarantees.

Your daughter won't bypass those normal teenage struggles. She may be hard-wired to oppose everything you want her to do, as Heather was. Psychologists use the term *oppositional* to describe such a child. Oppositional children seem to be in constant conflict with their parents and don't know what the word *cooperation* means. If you think your daughter may be an oppositional child, see if her behavior fits these characteristics adapted from a book by psychologist Norm Wright. The oppositional child:

- Enjoys being in control, so (she) challenges authority figures.
- Has a tendency to remain negative, even though the nega-tivism serves no purpose.
- Would rather compete than cooperate.
- Views right and wrong as somewhat relative.
- Is frustrating, since she doesn't respond to normal disci-pline techniques or approaches.[4]

As our journey with Heather progressed, I faced the reality that she was an oppositional child. I found it doesn't do any good to stick your head in the sand and pretend all is fine. Face the truth that your daughter will test you. Don't become passive and toss the tough situations to your wife or a counselor to handle. If you see the warning signs, become proactive. A mom told me her wayward daughter "never took the easy road." Your daughter may not take the easy road either.

Although it may seem odd, pray that your daughter goes through her difficult times before she can legally leave home. I've often thanked God that Heather's difficulties happened while she was still under my roof. Had they begun in young adulthood, my influence would have been diminished greatly. When I felt tempted to explode, I reminded myself that Heather's strong-willed nature, when it finally pointed in the right direction, would serve her well. Once she decided to do the right thing, that will would keep her on the right track. In that respect, being strong-willed was a positive.

3. Don't blow a gasket.

One of our counselors gave us wise insight into the word *offspring*. The common term, she said, suggests the truth that children will want to "spring off" from their parents to seek independence and form their own identities. That process of "springing off" came as a shock to Sherryl and me. We didn't have any experience with a child moving into adolescence. She was our firstborn, and we hadn't rebelled as teens, nor had our siblings.

I erred when I attempted to stifle Heather's desire for independence. She erred when she crossed the line of independence and stepped into rebellion. Dads, it helps to sort out the difference between our daughters' desire for independence and rebelliousness.

Mom's Tip

Mom, don't assume that your firstborn child will be your toughest child. That's not always the case. Allow God to use your intuition to discern each child's unique personality and respond accordingly.

Independence teaches our daughters to walk alone, whereas rebellion makes them refuse training, even when they can't walk alone.

When your daughter begins to change, it's okay to feel alarmed. Don't stay there, though. Our daughters need us to respond properly to their desire for more independence. We must recognize normal teenage problems for what they are and not overreact to them in any of these ways:

- Yelling, screaming, and calling them names.
- Grounding them until they're twenty-one.
- Banning them from church.
- Cutting them down in front of the family or friends.
- Passively ignoring them.
- Excluding them from family activities.
- Making doomsday forecasts (such as "You've now ruined your life forever.")
- Creating rules that guarantee their failure (for example, threatening no phone for six months if she leaves one more towel on the bathroom floor).

One of my early shocks came when Heather began to use bad language. I blew several gaskets at that point. I wish I'd applied this advice from David and Claudia Arp.

The early adolescent years (ages 12–14) often bring with them a fascination for dirty words and inappropriate sexual terms. If you accidentally find a filthy note, don't panic! You have not failed at parenthood. Do not take this note as evidence that your kid is into sex or drugs. If you found it legitimately, you can use it to open a discussion as to appropriate language, scriptural principles of sexuality, and controlling thoughts. But remember to listen, don't react![5]

The advice that I did heed came from our psychologist. He said, "Treat your daughter like she was somebody else's kid." Since I usually responded more calmly to another child's rebellion, this made sense. I reacted better to Heather's rebellion when I took his advice. This kept the tension between us manageable.

In the Bible, Timothy understood the power of a calm response when he wrote, "God's servant must not be argumentative, but a gentle listener and a teacher who keeps cool, working firmly but patiently with those who refuse to obey. You never know how or when God might sober them up with a change of heart and a turning to the truth" (2 Timothy 2:24–25, MSG).

Finally, if your daughter comes home with a stick-on tattoo (or a real one), pink hair, or punk-rock clothes, remember the battles with your dad over long hair, the Rolling Stones, and bell-bottoms.

4. Balance toughness with tenderness.

This choice becomes a delicate balancing act. Psychologist John White puts it this way:

> Where is the fine line between troublesome behavior that will sort itself out eventually and the signs of an approaching hurricane? I don't have a clear answer, but when we make a conscious effort to balance control with freedom, it will pay off.[6]

Discover your tendency—too tough or too tender. I asked one mother what she wished she had done differently with her rebellious daughter. Without hesitation she said, "I'd have been tougher on her with her friends." I asked why she wasn't. With remorse she said, "I was afraid she would run."

When our kids sense our fears and we become too permissive, they can use those fears to intimidate us. They can threaten to disrupt our lives if we hold them accountable. If fear of your daughter's actions tend to drive your decisions, become more firm with her.

On the other hand, if you try to control your daughter with an iron hand, you may need to lighten up. If you become too controlling with a rigid set of "biblical principles," you might keep her under control. In the long run, however, you can harm the relationship. She'll resent your attempts to control her.

Striking a balance between toughness and tenderness will challenge you. As you work toward that balance, you help preserve the relationship with your daughter. Steve Arterburn describes a famous Rembrandt painting of the prodigal son that illustrates this balance.

> If you look at that painting you will notice the hands of the father on the back of the prodigal boy. The hands are very different because for one Rembrandt used a female model and for the other he used a strong male. The soft hand of the female represents God's tender mercy and forgiveness. The strong hand represents the tough love that must be there for every prodigal. Strength and grace—the perfect combination to parent a prodigal.[7]

5. Minimize other negative factors that may contribute to your daughter's problems.

Miles McPherson parallels the battle a difficult child goes through to the "physical battle that people experience when destructive cancer cells take over a normally healthy body."[8] He says we must find out where the "cancer originated and from where it continues to draw support."[9]

In retrospect, we now realize several outside factors contributed to our struggle with Heather. Our youngest daughter, Tiffany, faced three brain surgeries as Heather approached adolescence. During that time Tiffany got most of our attention, and we unknowingly neglected Heather's emotional needs. She wrote in one of her journals, "I feel so alone, like when you took Tiffany to Baltimore [for a surgery]."

Another incident at her Christian school fueled the coming crises. A boy made very disparaging comments about her body. Although we did complain, the boy received only a slap on the hand from administrators because his mother was a teacher. This appeared unfair to Heather, and she didn't feel that we stood up for her.

Every family faces unique challenges. Check the factors from this list that might add stress to your daughter's life. If she faces one or more of these issues, find ways to minimize their impact on her.

❑ Low self-esteem
❑ Rejection by peers
❑ Unrealistic expectations from parents
❑ Overly busy parents who are absent or uninvolved
❑ Parents' struggling marriage
❑ Divorce in the family
❑ Childhood abuse
❑ Constant relocation
❑ Perceived hypocrisy of parents or the church community
❑ Prolonged sickness of a family member
❑ Death of a close relative
❑ Alcohol or drug abuse
❑ Unmonitored access to cable TV and the Internet

Raising your daughter may prove the most challenging task you've ever faced. It was for me. As we began our journey, though, I made a commitment to God. I told him, "Lord, while Heather is under our roof, I want to give her every opportunity to turn back to You. One day when I stand before You I want to hear You say this about my parenting: 'Well done, good and faithful servant.'"

The pain and frustration overwhelmed me at times. But I've

often asked myself if the extra effort was worth it. My answer? A resounding *yes!*

Pay the price to steer your daughter in the right direction. Don't panic. Persevere for the long haul, and realize that small decisions you make today can profoundly impact your daughter's future for the good. You never know—she may one day buy you a John Deere mower.

Relationship Lifters

- At an appropriate time in the next three days, ask your daughter if she senses increased tension between the two of you. Listen with your heart. Ask her what she'd like you to change in your behavior to lessen the tension.
- Leave a note for your daughter. Write with feeling how much you love her. Ask her to write you a note back to include any observations about a time or times in which you reacted to, something she did. (Don't expect it to be a love note, though).
- Ask your daughter if other factors in her life currently cause her stress, and ask her how you can help. Follow through!
- Ask your wife to tell you honestly if you tend to be tough or tender. Make a list of three changes you can begin to make this week to become more balanced. Tell your daughter about the changes you plan to make.

For Daughters

I trembled as I clutched the note. My entire body flushed, and I went numb with shame. I felt pins and needles from head to toe. The angry knot forming in the pit of my stomach burned like acid.

The tears I tried to fight back blurred the words on the page as time stood still.

What I read wasn't what any girl wanted to hear from all the boys she'd known since she was ten. But the poem and the tasteless pictures that comprised the note I received from the boys in my eighth-grade class became a milestone in my life—a bad one.

Since the fourth grade, I had attended the same Christian school ... and I was a *nerd*. When long, blonde, crimped hair was "cool," I had a strange, mouse-colored bowl cut that frizzed in the back. Plastic dangly hoop earrings that should have stayed in the eighties hung from my ears. I had buck teeth and pale skin, and I was gangly: one boy compared me to a flamingo. I brought new meaning to the phrase "the awkward stage." In addition to these strikes against me, I committed social suicide: I wore my *mother's clothes*. I am not kidding.

I was also a straight-A student and the unanimous teachers' pet. Teachers adored me, but I was obnoxious to the other students. Even before a question left the teacher's mouth, my hand shot up. I always gave the long version of the right answer, and I corrected the students who answered incorrectly. Being a good student wasn't my problem; being a show-off was.

While I may have appeared pleased with my intelligence and my popularity with the faculty, I wasn't. I was lonely. I had no friends, and I always felt like the butt of everyone's jokes. I hated being the outsider.

As I grew older, I realized that my current habits wouldn't increase my popularity, so I tried to change. I thought I improved my fashion choices. (No more searching in Mom's closet.) I let my hair grow longer, though it was just a longer bowl cut. I got new shoes and a new green sweater that I thought complemented my figure. I began to wear mascara and a little bit of lipstick. And I finally wore a bra, though I didn't really need one. (I stuffed it.) I felt better about myself. I knew I was nerdy and socially awkward, but I eagerly hoped to change things. I just wanted friends.

But then, the unfolded piece of paper that lay on my desk shattered everything.

> Roses are red,
> Violets are black,
> Your chest is as flat
> As my white back.

I was floored. I thought my classmates had stopped laughing at me. I thought people were treating me better. I thought I had begun forming a few friendships. I was wrong. The note meant that I was still a nobody—and that realization crushed me. The note cut me to the core of my being. In that instant, I imagined the entire class turning to look at me, pointing at me, and taunting me. I felt vulnerable, miserable, and totally alone.

That note was a significant turning point for me. I rid myself of the idea of being friends with those people. And they were supposed to be Christians. I began to write off Christians in general, and then God. *I've had it,* I thought. *It's over.*

Another significant event in my life occurred after that tumultuous eighth-grade year that involved the church youth group's annual trip to Six Flags over Georgia for its Christian concert weekend.

The school year was over, and I tried to forget the note. I felt I was beginning to come into my own. Maybe it wasn't coming into my own as much as it was my determination to be "cool." I began identifying myself with the skater crowd. I grew out my hair (from the scary bowl cut) and dyed tiny streaks of it blue with Kool-Aid. I started shopping at thrift stores. I bought my first pair of Etnies shoes.

That summer the church youth group (which I was reluctantly still a part of) decided to take a four-day trip to Six Flags. I went with my friend Anne, a.k.a. my best friend and partner in crime. We highlighted all the "alternative" bands' concerts. (We weren't going to be caught dead watching Steven Curtis Chapman!) We decided to ride the rides during the day and attend the shows at night.

On the second night, Anne and I sat on the top bleacher, head-banging, which was our way to show how "cool" we were. We noticed three cute boys standing next to us, so we began head-banging more noticeably. Finally, she dared me to turn to one and ask, "Where is the Hoi Polloi concert?"

The dare resulted in success. They commented how they'd never seen girls headbanging, but that it was really cool. (Apparently, they were just as misinformed about what was "cool" as we were.) We flirted with each other for the rest of the night. After the concerts finished, we agreed to meet the next morning.

I felt incredible. A boy actually showed interest in me! This was a new experience. After the rough year I'd had and all the verbal blows I'd taken about my appearance, a boy found me attractive. It was intoxicating. And it definitely bolstered my almost extinct self-esteem.

The next day, we rode rides, played games, and paid to have our caricatures drawn. As we walked around the park, someone (I'm sure it was one of the boys) suggested, "Hey! Let's go on Monster Plantation!" Monster Plantation was a boat ride through a kids' haunted mansion.

Anne and I looked at each other wide-eyed and unanimously said, "Okay." Monster Plantation was slow and dark. We all knew what that meant: *kissing*.

We hopped on the ride. After a few minutes of purple monsters stirring pots of witches' brew, the ride slowed and everything went pitch-black. Then, the inevitable happened.

It didn't matter that it felt as if I had a banana slug in my mouth or that I feared I would choke on his tongue—he kissed me! I was elated. A cute boy (without any apparent psychological problems) took an interest in flat-chested, skinny me. I was walking on clouds the rest of the trip.

During our last two days, Anne and I went everywhere with our Six Flags "boyfriends." They won us stuffed dogs and bought us overpriced Cokes. We held hands as we walked around the park. We had photo-booth pictures taken with the boys. As we walked back to the campers where the youth group stayed, Anne and I whispered excitedly about our day's adventures.

When the time came to part with our temporary boyfriends, Anne and I were depressed. They lived hours away and we were too young to drive, so we exchanged phone numbers and addresses and agreed to write.

When I got home the next morning, I could hardly wait to tell someone about my exciting trip. So who else would I call but my good friend Chelsea? *Big mistake.* As I recounted every detail of the past four days' events, neither of us heard her mom pick up the phone—and listen to part of our conversation. After her mom grilled her, she caved and told her everything.

The following day, my world came crashing down. Her mom called my mom and told her what she'd heard from Chelsea. My mom then told my dad. I was utterly unprepared for his reaction. To make a long story short, my dad accused me of wanting to be a prostitute and called the boy's father to report the incident (which his dad thought was no big deal). He also talked to my Six Flags boyfriend and warned him to stay away from me, then grounded me for two weeks. My mom bawled during the whole thing.

I plodded up to my room, dumbfounded and defeated. In my entire thirteen years, I had never been grounded. My dad had never really yelled at me before. I only kissed the boy. I could have understood a reaction like that if perhaps we were trying to hook up in the youth group camper, but we only kissed and held hands!

These two incidents jump-started my downward spiral. The vicious humiliation the note caused tore me apart. When I felt that I had finally met a guy who liked me and made me feel okay about my looks, my personality, and everything else I was insecure about, my best friend betrayed me and my dad went crazy with his reaction.

I never willingly talked to Chelsea again. Yet I thought, *More "Christian principles" that are turning around and biting me in the backside.* Then my dad—the pastor—eliminated from my life the one guy that made me feel accepted. This ignited my anger at my dad . . . and at God. I thought, *Forget this. I've already endured torment at the hands of these "Christian" boys. Then my "Christian" friend rats me out. My dad grounds me for two weeks for something that I don't feel bad about and says it's against "Christian principles." I've had it with God . . . and I've had it with Dad.*

Perhaps you've endured a similar situation. Maybe you weren't made fun of growing up, or you were never punished for kissing boys. Perhaps your crisis is something completely different. Take comfort: you're not alone. However, don't make the same mistakes I did. Give some of the following ideas a try, and maybe you'll avoid the messes I made.

Manage your anger.

I misdirected my anger. My anger at the boys who made fun of me and at the kissing incident spilled over onto other areas of my life. I let my angry reaction to these two significant, painful events cloud my judgment. My reactionary, impulsive choices led me down a painful road for the next five years.

Anger in itself isn't wrong. It's a natural emotion, just like sadness, happiness, fearfulness, and so on. However, it's what you do with your anger that determines its rightness or wrongness.

Ephesians 4:26 says, "In your anger do not sin." Don't let your anger color your world: keep it under control.

Don't assume; communicate.

I felt that my dad should have dealt more harshly with the note incident. The ringleader and author of the note got only a "talking to" from the principal since his mom taught at the school. I was furious! I felt that I had been treated unjustly not only by the "Christian" students but by the "Christian" faculty. I also felt that my dad, who was supposed to be my protector, didn't follow-up enough. He now tells me that he never realized I felt that way— because I never told him.

Don't assume your dad can read your mind. He understands you probably as well as you understand the intake valves in a car. (I don't even know what they are.) Tell him the straight facts. I never discussed the kissing incident with my dad—he grounded me, I got mad, and from that point on, I made him the enemy. He did overreact, but I did, too. Remember, dads don't like boys to be within ten yards of their daughters—especially those who want to kiss their daughters. Maybe he thought I was trying to make some fast cash at the corner of the Viper and the Scream Machine. Well, not really, but .... I should have made sure my dad had the story straight. Make sure your dad knows the facts. Don't be the victim of hearsay.

Find someone to help you keep your head on straight.

During my crazy years, there was someone who never stopped praying for me, loving me, accepting me, and communicating with me. That someone was a lady at my church named Mrs. Dietz. Though I shocked her with much of what I told her, she did her best to conceal her surprise and gave me excellent advice. More importantly, she was there for me whenever I needed her. Only in retrospect do I understand what an important part of my life she truly was. She modeled what the Bible says about a true friend: "A friend loves at all times" (Proverbs 17:17).

She may never know it, but her influence still profoundly influences my life. Find yourself a Mrs. Dietz, someone older and wiser to talk to and confide in.

Remember: this is new to your dad.

I went from Bibles, Christian T-shirts, and youth group activities to pink hair, Doc Martens, and punk-rock shows in a matter of a few months. My dad didn't know what happened. So cut your dad some slack. If he overreacts to your choice of music or your curfew requests, allow him that. Be patient with him. Compromise, compromise, compromise.

What if you came home from school one day, and your dad had gotten his lip pierced, dyed his hair black, and was talking about good "emo" music? Imagine how frightened and confused you'd feel! Well, your dad could be going through the same emotions because of the changes you're making. Go easy on him.

You don't have to let your relationship with your dad dwindle to nearly nothing as I did. Life is easier when you keep your dad active in your life. He was a boy once (back when they still rode in horse-drawn carriages), and he can give you valuable advice about guys. While I used to sneak around with my boyfriends, now I sometimes tell Dad to try to scare them away. When I need advice about money matters, jobs, school, and so on, I go to my dad. He can be a very valuable asset in your life—so don't mess up what you've got!

As long as you keep your anger under control and keep

communication open with your dad, you can spare yourself many of the difficulties I faced during my teenage years.

Relationship Lifters

- Set a few times a month to go on "dates" with your dad, but make them reasonable. (Don't ask him to go to a tattoo parlor to get matching tattoos.) Don't let him become a stranger to you.
- Let your dad into your world. Let him listen to some of your music. Tell him about some of the things you like to do. Tell him why. He might not understand, but making the effort to keep him informed about your life will mean a lot to him and will strengthen your relationship.
- Find yourself a person to confide in (like my Mrs. Dietz). Find someone at your church, someone you trust, someone older and wiser. Ask her if you can go to her when you need someone to talk to. If you feel uncomfortable talking to your parents, go to that person for advice.

Mom to Mom

When Heather began to rebel, I was in the dark. One day after church as I chatted with friends, Heather sauntered by and sneered, "I used to want to look like you, act like you, and be like you, but those days are over." With that, she turned on her heels and left me speechless and broken.

Only later did I understand that hurt people hurt people. I know now her words were evidence that pain boiled beneath her veneer. I wish I had come alongside her to talk about her world. Unfortunately, I didn't. Instead I began to emotionally distance myself from her to protect myself from further pain. Mom, if your daughter begins to hurt you, stay emotionally connected. I know it hurts, but don't pull away.

As I fought the temptation to pull away, I realized how important it was to keep the lines of communication open with Charles. We were clueless about how we should respond to Heather and how to manage the emotional drain on both of us. In those early years, we often reacted to the smallest acts of rebellion. This response created tension in our marriage.

We finally called a truce and admitted we didn't know what to do. We started to fervently pray and began to work as a unified team. If you sense that rough times with your daughter lie ahead, get away with your husband for uninterrupted time. Talk about your feelings and commit to work together as a team.

A Mother's Prayer

O Perfect Father,
I need Your grace, wisdom, and strength
to parent my child.
I cannot do it without You.
Help me to see her with Your eyes
and love her with Your heart.
Please help my husband and me
to work together in
Your Spirit's power.

two

VERBAL VENOM

At this juncture in a man's life, he realizes he
doesn't have much control over his kids.
— Entry in Charles Stone's Journal,
December 29, 1996

For Dads

As tension with Heather continued to mount, angry words began
to fly in both directions. As a pastor I had often taught that careless words could easily become destructive weapons. My relationship with Heather forced me to decide if I could walk my talk. My
heart still aches when I think about one incident when I crushed
Heather with my words. I wish I could take it back. Dads, don't do
what I did; learn from my mistake.

As Heather's rebellion worsened the first year of our journey,
she developed a close relationship with a friend in our church's
youth group. They talked on the phone, often spent lots of time
together, and shared secrets. Unfortunately, the trust she built with
her friend was soon shattered.

The summer after the tattoo incident, the church youth group
attended a Christian concert weekend at the amusement park Six
Flags over Georgia. At that time Heather's behavior hadn't deteriorated to the point that we worried about her. One of the leaders
on the trip even remarked how Heather set a good example for the

other youth. However, a few days after the trip, my wife received a disturbing phone call from the mother of Heather's friend. She explained that her daughter had confided in her about an incident between Heather and a boy she had met on the trip. The mom then shared the graphic details.

I knew that the Six Flags Christian weekend featured several Christian concerts. I assumed someone like Glen Campbell would sing with perhaps a brass ensemble or local church choir to accompany him. Was I surprised as Sherryl explained that the music at this concert led Heather to "headbang." I didn't exactly know what "headbanging" meant, but it didn't sound good. Glen Campbell would never allow that at one of his concerts. No rhinestone cowboy would ever stoop that low. Because of what Sherryl told me next, I figured it must have been some sort of mating call, as when peacocks spread their tail feathers. As a result of this headbanging incident, Heather struck up a friendship with a boy she didn't know. They clicked and decided to hang out for the rest of the weekend.

Then my wife reported the shocking result of this headbanging. Heather k-i-s-s-e-d that I-like-girls-who-headbang boy! My thirteen-year-old daughter had smooched with a stranger from who-knows-where.

At the moment my wife described that kiss, I immediately reacted in her presence with a self-righteous diatribe on moral purity, venereal disease, sex in movies, Pet Rocks, Chia pets, and anything else I was ticked off about. (Stupid mistake.) You would have thought that she had had sex with the guy. Fortunately, Heather was at a friend's house at the time.

I had to release my volcano of self-righteous emotions, and it wasn't "spiritually correct" to yell at my wife. (I'm a pastor, remember?) My black cockapoo, innocently watching this scenario, would not have appreciated a kick either. So, I dashed up to Heather's room to look for more evidence of her moral-corruption-that-would- certainly-result-in-pregnancy-out-of-wedlock. I frantically yanked open drawers, jerked furniture from the walls, and plundered her book bag. No evidence yet. Then, taking a clue from a *Columbo* show, I lifted her mattress and found the irrefutable evidence of this "Godforsaken" act of sexual immorality: her diary.

I quickly thumbed through it to the entry that described the Six Flags incident. (Very stupid mistake.) There it was, in black and white: a blow-by-blow account of this terrible act of unrighteousness. She really kissed the guy, several times, and she wrote that she liked it. That horrific news further stoked my anger. I rushed downstairs with fire in my eyes, and with staccato-like precision, filled my wife's ears with doomsday predictions of Heather's future unless we brought her to repent of this immoral act.

> *Mom's Tip*
>
> Mom, sometimes you must respectfully, but forcefully, put your foot down with your husband. If he begins to overreact to your daughter, have him cool down several hours *before* he confronts her.

Dads, please keep perspective when this happens. My daughter had only kissed the boy. That was it! I was way over the top.

I sat in the cushioned white wicker chair in front of our home's sunroom window. That gave me a full view of our front yard, and I wanted to see Heather before she walked inside. As I stewed, I locked and loaded my verbal M-16 with heart-penetrating ammo to kill the root of the cancer I assumed grew in her heart.

Then I saw her run happily toward the garage that led directly into the sunroom. I waited like a cat ready to pounce on a hapless sparrow. What happened next still brings pangs of guilt.

As she opened the garage door, she immediately saw my beady eyes and furrowed brows. Her face fell. She asked, "What's wrong, Dad?"

"What's wrong? I'll tell you what's wrong!" I yelled in my

firmest God voice. "This is wrong." I jabbed her diary at her face with a Zorro-like flair.

Heather began to retreat into the house the way a child threatened by a grizzly would. As her face became ashen, she slowly collapsed to the floor in fear and shock at my fury. She leaned her back against our roll-top desk. I stood a good five feet over Heather at that point, as she rolled into a tight fearful ball.

"We know what you did with that boy. I can't believe you'd stoop to such immorality," I snarled in a bellicose tone. (A little too much "tough love" here, you think?)

And then these words dripped off my tongue like acid. *"Do... you... want... to... become... a... prostitute?"*

I wish I could forever take back those hateful words, but I can't.

I had yielded to the temptation many dads face. We sometimes believe that only strong words, a harsh tone, and our authority can motivate our daughters to change. Seldom does that style succeed.

In retrospect I fully realize my tongue deeply wounded her soul. I believe those cutting words contributed to the five years of turmoil we experienced with her. Although I later apologized, my words that day became weapons that damaged our relationship. As another parent wrote in a similar situation, I felt "the pain of witnessing the hurt of someone my anger has needlessly wounded and of knowing I am destroying a relationship that is precious to me."[1]

I had failed to heed Paul's advice in Ephesians 4:26, where he wrote, "In your anger do not sin." Instead, my outburst mimicked the observation King Solomon made in Proverbs, "Reckless words pierce like a sword" (12:18).

A dad's reckless words can become verbal venom that will poison his relationship with his daughter. I saw a perfect parallel of this when I channel-surfed one evening and found a nature show about a man who raised cobras for show. He had agreed to let a TV production company tape how he handled these deadly snakes. His father was watching the taping.

The snake handler carried the snakes in plastic storage containers much like the ones we use to store clothes under our bed. With the tape rolling, he grabbed the snake by its tail, held it out as far as he could, opened the container, and dropped the snake in headfirst. He usually kept about two feet between himself and the storage container.

As he put the snake into the container with his right hand, he held the container lid with his left hand. At the moment he released the snake's tail, he dropped the lid onto the container. Only one time the cobra had twisted around in the box with its head aimed at the handler. Before the box top closed, the snake uncoiled and struck at the handler, barely nicking him in the stomach.

It retreated into the box, and the handler secured the lid. But the clock began to tick as the tiny yet potent amount of venom began to seep into his bloodstream. The handler then nonchalantly lifted his shirt to look at the two bite marks. As he stared at his wound, he matter-of-factly told his dad, "We'd better get to the hospital, quick."

On the thirty-minute drive to the hospital, the camera caught the son describing his searing pain and difficulty breathing. "I don't know if I'm going to make it. I'd better call my wife," he said to his father. With labored breath he told his wife what happened and said, "I may not make it. I love you."

The emergency room immediately administered massive amounts of anti-venom. The camera zoomed in on a rapidly growing hole in the man's stomach as the venom literally ate away his flesh. The handler survived, but his stomach scar would always remind him of the venom's destructive power.

The biblical writer James used a similar image when he wrote that our tongues can become "a restless evil, full of deadly poison" (James 3:8). The original language in this passage refers to a snake slithering up alongside its victim, unnoticed. Then the snake strikes, injects its venom, and slithers away into the grass. In a similar way, reckless words can deposit venom into a relationship and destroy it, just as the cobra's poison destroyed the flesh of the snake handler. One parent wrote after she used words as weapons, "I can't bear the way she [her daughter] looks at me—hurt and scared. And I know I've done it again. I've destroyed a bit more of her."[2]

❧——❧

Until I experienced the opposite, I believed this familiar childhood maxim: Sticks and stone may break my bones, but words will never hurt me. Dads, perhaps you, too, believed it until you felt the sting of a cutting comment from your own father or a sarcastic jab from a friend. The Bible contradicts this childhood fallacy.

Perhaps the strongest statement about our words comes from Proverbs 18:21: "The tongue has the power of life and death." The word *power* actually comes from the Hebrew word for "hand." When I unloaded those caustic words on Heather, it hurt her as much as if I'd slapped her. It sapped life from our relationship. Later, when I used my tongue wisely, it brought life into our relationship. I learned that the quality of my communication with Heather correlated with the health of our relationship.

> ### Mom's Tip
>
> Mom, share with your husband when someone misused his or her words against you. Describe how it made you feel, and encourage him to not let his words hurt your daughter's soul.

Proverbs 18:21 ends with "Those who love it will eat its fruit." Solomon wisely observed that our words will yield fruit: the fruit of relational life or relational death. He also gave sage advice about our words elsewhere in Proverbs.

When words are many, sin is not absent,
but he who holds his tongue is wise. (10:19)

Reckless words pierce like a sword,
but the tongue of the wise brings healing. (12:18)

The tongue that brings healing is a tree of life,
but a deceitful tongue crushes the spirit. (15:4)

Pleasant words are a honeycomb,
sweet to the soul and healing to the bones. (16:24)

He who answers before listening—
that is his folly and his shame. (18:13)

James further described our tongue's power with a few memo-
rable images in the third chapter of his epistle. He likened our
tongues to a bit in a horse's mouth and to a ship's rudder. Although
small, a rudder and a bit wield great power to control something
much larger. Our words carry great power to determine the course
of a dad-daughter relationship.

James also described our tongues as a small spark that can set an
entire forest on fire. Almost every year huge wildfires rage in the
West. These begin with a cigarette thrown carelessly out a car
window or a tiny ember left in a campfire. As a result, fires leave
thousands of homes and hundreds of thousands of acres in piles of
ash. Likewise, our words can scorch our relationships with our
daughters. One careless word can easily turn a simple disagreement
into a full-blown verbal inferno. The Message says, "A sharp tongue
kindles a temper-fire" (Proverbs 15:1).

How to Apply Relational Life Preserver 2

1. Convince yourself that your daughter does want to talk to you, even though she may not admit it.

Scott Larson, an expert on difficult parent-teen relationships, writes,

> Many parents wonder if their kids really want their help. Believe me—they do. One major study revealed that while kids do go to each other first for advice, they don't trust it. Overwhelmingly, the youth surveyed indicated they would prefer to go to their parents or other adults first, but they did not believe they had a relationship with them that allowed them to talk openly about their problems.[3]

Heather's words and actions often conveyed that she could have cared less if we communicated. Unfortunately, because I believed it, sometimes I didn't make the extra effort to keep the communication lines open. We need to know our daughters need us, and our daughters need to know that we know.

2. Let your daughter vent without lecturing her.

Resist the temptation to correct every poor choice or angry word your daughter utters. Let her vent her emotions when she needs to. Sometimes even let her have the last word.

This brings to mind an incident not with Heather but with my youngest daughter, Tiffany. She battles the aftereffects of brain surgery—the loss of some short-term memory that impacts her school performance. One day, on the way back from a doctor's appointment, she blurted out, "I hate my algebra teacher!"

I knew she didn't hate him. Her teacher had failed to account for her limitations and had lowered her grade. At that moment she didn't need platitudes; she needed to express her anger and disappointment. But I blew it. "Jesus doesn't want us to hate people," I admonished her.

What I should have done was place my hand on her shoulder and say, "Tiffany, I'm so sorry. I know how much it must hurt when things like this happen. I love you with all my heart. How can I help?"

I've learned that when a daughter says something extreme, often her frustration rather than her better judgment controls what she is saying. Her anger can be a symptom of inner pain that needs a listening ear rather than a lecture. Otherwise, she may act like a box turtle I kept as a kid. When he felt the least bit threatened, he'd pull his head into his shell and wouldn't stick it out again until he felt it safe to do so.

3. Zip your lips when you feel angry.

I reacted too often to Heather's angry words with my own. When I did, I put a kink in the lifeline of communication, much like what happened in some of the old deep-sea diving movies. The diver, many fathoms below the water's surface, relied on the hose to provide oxygen to keep him alive. If something put a kink in the line, the lack of oxygen would quickly kill him.

Both King David in the Old Testament and James in the New Testament gave advice on how to defuse a volatile situation and avoid a relational risk. "Take control of what I say, O LORD, and keep my lips sealed" (Psalm 141:3 NLT). "My dear brothers and sisters, be quick to listen, slow to speak and slow to get angry" (James 1:19 NLT).

I also learned to heed the wisdom of people like Thomas Jefferson, who wrote, "When angry, count to ten before you speak; if very angry, count to a hundred." This helped calm me down, and still does. It gives me time to formulate "I" messages ("I feel sad," "I feel frustrated") instead of "you" messages ("You always . . . ," "You make me . . ."). Heather always responded more favorably to "I" messages than "you" messages. Dad, our goal is to avoid words that we regret after it is too late. Once spoken, an angry word can't be taken back.

At the same time, driving anger inward without appropriate expression can be as damaging as exploding verbally. As Dr. Norman Wright observes,

> Learning to release your anger in a healthy manner can affect your life in a positive way. You have a choice. Repressing or suppressing anger is like carrying a gun which is loaded and cocked. Eventually it will go off and somebody will get hurt. But releasing anger constructively defuses the ammunition and empties the gun.[4]

4. Watch for open windows of opportunity to communicate with your daughter. They won't last long.

Most of my good conversations with Heather during the teen years came in sound bites of thirty to sixty seconds. If I stayed lost in my own world, I missed those crucial moments to talk. But when I stayed sensitive to the Holy Spirit in those teachable moments and responded by listening, we connected and our relationship strengthened.

So plan ahead and be watchful. David and Claudia Arp suggest this: "Think ahead through major issues, and prepare thirty-second mental outlines of your thoughts for those rare occasions when your adolescents ask for your wisdom."[5]

5. Speak positive words to your daughter even when you don't feel like it.

Dads, I know how you feel when your daughters seem to do everything wrong. When that happens, it's tough to find anything good to say. However, these three words will fit even the worst situation: *I love you.*

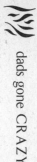

I don't think we can overuse that phrase with our kids, although my son Josh informed us when he was nineteen that we did. I have ignored his comment and still tell him I love him at least once a day.

Aside from "I love you," make a list of qualities that you appreciate about your daughter. Write them down, and keep the list with you. When she blows it, pull out the list, and at the appropriate time, speak positive words into your daughter's heart. We all need affirmation because "studies indicate that it takes fourteen affirming statements to overcome a single negative one."[6]

When you apply this chapter's relational life preserver, one day you will experience deep joy when you connect with your daughter's heart.

RELATIONSHIP LIFTERS

- What words have you spoken to your daughter this week out of anger? Go ask for her forgiveness, and don't give excuses.
- Ask your daughter to tell you honestly how well she thought you listened to her during the past three days. Ask her what you should do differently to become a better listener.
- Each day next week, write one positive quality you see in your daughter on a sticky note. Stick it on her bathroom mirror before she goes to school. Also, make "I love you" a regular part of your vocabulary.
- Ask your wife to critique how you respond during the next crisis with your daughter. Based on her observations, what will you do differently next time?

For Daughters

My relationship with my dad began to really fall apart after my Six Flags experience. He didn't trust me. I began to hang around with friends who influenced me to make dumb choices, including smoking pot and more. That fall I was kicked out of two Christian schools because of my behavior. Things deteriorated to the point that my parents sent me to a local hospital with a rehab unit for wild kids. I hated the weeks I stayed there and vowed never to return. But nothing I was doing changed, and I hit another wall. I'll never forget what happened a few weeks after my first stay at the center.

I shot up from my bed in anger and disbelief. "What?" I yelled. As my parents stood in front of me in my room, they informed me that they were sending me back to the treatment center. My predictable response to bad news, or anything else I took even a minor disliking to, was about to follow: no fewer insults and expletives than you'd hear on an Eminem CD.

They left, and immediately I grabbed my phone and called one of my friends to come rescue me. A few minutes later, my parents returned to my room to check on me—they knew I would try something crazy. I was seething. I began screaming as they frantically tried to calm me down. Then, a small voice from outside got my attention.

"Hey! Hey!"

I ran to my window and looked out. A stranger stood on the sidewalk below me.

She said, "Are you Heather?"

"Yes!"

"They're here—let's go!"

I spied the maroon car parked up the street. I vowed, *I'm gone.* With my adrenaline pumping, I knocked my mom onto the floor. My dad tried to block me in the doorway, but I barreled past him like an angry bull. I had been in rehab before, and I was *not* going back.

I bounded down the stairs three and four at a time. I flung open the front door and ran, with my dad hot on my trail. It was as if someone fired a gun into the air and shouted, "They're off!" As we raced through the front yards of our quiet neighborhood, we must have looked ridiculous. I tried to hold down my miniskirt as I sprinted toward the car—my green knee-high, steel-toed Doc Martens made running quite difficult.

With his cell phone in hand, my father chased me as he continued to scream, "Stop, Heather! Stop! *Stop!*" I later found out that he was attempting to dial 9-1-1. (Fortunately, you must push "Send" in order to call the number. My father did not. To me, this was further proof that old people—such as my father—are not meant to use modern devices, meaning anything invented after the 1930s).

I could hear him panting. His feet pounded behind me. I ran over a hill, jumped over curbs, and trampled the neighbors' flower beds. Breathless, I reached the car and yelled, "Drive!" even before I grabbed the door handle and scrambled in. Too late. My dad blocked the car and waved his cell phone threateningly at me. I shouted to the driver, "Run him over! Go!" And I meant it. I stopped only when my dad yelled, "I've memorized the car's license plate number, and the police are on their way!" (I guess he did finally push that "Send" button.)

I didn't surrender and get out of the car because I cared whether the car hit him. I got out only because I didn't want my friends to get busted. Trembling with anger, I told my friends I'd see them soon and slammed the door. I was in a rage. I began screaming "$%*#@ you! $%*#@ you!"—and anything else that would hurt and embarrass my father—at the top of my lungs. Our whole neighborhood must have heard.

I stormed back to my house, bellowing threats and insults. In my desperation, out of the garage I grabbed . . . garden tools. Yes, that's right. Rakes, shovels, hedge trimmers, and whatever else I could find. Still screaming obscenities, I took the tools (though I couldn't have told you what they were used for to save my life) and began to throw them at our house. Perhaps my neighbors thought this was my unconventional way of trimming the bushes. I was a sight, throwing rakes at my house in my miniskirt and green boots and screaming at my father.

When the cops finally arrived, they threatened me with juvenile hall, then called an ambulance and transported me back to the rehab. I ended up in the place I tried so hard to avoid.

This was a not-so-unusual day in my life. My greatest regret today isn't the treatment center or the cops; it is that each word I said to my dad buried itself in his heart like a bullet. With every curse, every threat, every "I hate you!" I wounded my dad's spirit.

Obviously, this was one of many instances when I allowed my angry words to push my dad and me farther apart. For most of my teen years, the only words I used with my dad were cutting, mean, and hateful. Rarely did I use my words to repair or further our relationship. I used my mouth like a verbal machine gun.

James, author of the book in the Bible that's named after him, wrote about the power of our words. He compared our tongues (among other things) to a bit in a horse's mouth.

I can relate to this analogy. When I used to ride horses, Sugar, a fat, white Arabian, was my favorite. Why? Because she was feisty. When you least expected it, she'd turn around to bite your leg. She would purposefully gallop under low tree branches to knock the rider off her back. If she got really aggravated, she wouldn't quit bucking until the helpless rider flew off.

I enjoyed Sugar because she was a challenge to control. No

matter how many times I rode, it never failed to amaze me how the bit, only a three-inch piece of metal, could control this stubborn, fifteen-hundred-pound horse. When I used a soft touch on the reins, which meant a gentle pull on the bit, she seemed to thank me by her obedience. Because she was such a difficult horse, however, many times riders lost patience with her and jerked on the reins. When this happened, she became angry and began to bite or buck. Sugar's cooperation depended upon the rider's use of the bit in her mouth.

This also applies to the words we use. King Solomon wrote, "A gentle response defuses ange" (Proverbs 15:1 MSG). When I used my words as weapons against my father, it only added bricks to the growing wall that separated us. Though your dad may not show it, it hurts him to hear that you don't like him or even hate him. But gentle, considerate words can encourage your dad and strengthen your relationship. Positive words serve as the "bit" that turns the relationship in the right direction.

You can use words as building blocks or weapons, bridges or bullets. Force yourself not to roll your eyes or say something mean; listen to him. When I mouthed off to my dad, I only made things worse for myself. Choose wisely.

I learned a few ways to make communication easier between me and my dad. Try them out—maybe they'll work for you too.

Don't speak.

This is a huge problem I faced with my dad. I refused to listen to him. And I *always* had to have the last word. Even after the conversation was finished, I'd say, "Whatever" or "Yeah, sure" in my most sarcastic tone just so I could "win" the argument. But really, I was losing whatever open communication my dad and I had. Listen to your dad; don't use the time he speaks to you to formulate your comeback. Respect what he has to say by listening, and I bet he'll show you that respect, too.

Show him you're listening.

I had the attitude thing down to a science. As soon as my dad said, "Heather, I'd like to see you in my office" (which was code for "You're in a lot of trouble"), my performance began. I stomped down the stairs loudly. I entered the doorway and tossed him the I-don't-care-what-you're-about-to-say glance. I sauntered over to the chair, sat with a thud, and sighed as loudly and annoyingly as possible. At that point, I stared out the window for the duration of the "talk."

Perhaps your body language isn't as exaggerated as mine was, but you know what I'm talking about. Don't do it! Show your dad you're listening by nixing the charades. Also, his lectures will probably be a lot shorter. Dads tend to ramble even more when they're agitated.

Think about what you say
before you say it.

This is exactly what I did *not* do. I said many things to my father that I wish I could erase. In my anger, I said things that were like a verbal slap on his face. Avoid this at all costs—think about what you say before you say it. Don't let cruel words leave your mouth in a fit of rage. Take a deep breath, count to ten, or run out the back door and scream (which I did). Do whatever is necessary to calm down and collect your thoughts; then speak. Don't let the heat of the moment get the best of you. Don't make angry words your first reaction.

Apologize.

This was the hardest part for me. I was often too prideful to admit I was wrong and apologize to my father. But those three small words—*I am sorry*—have so much power to heal. When you say something vicious out of anger or frustration, apologize. Do it in your own time so that it's sincere—it will be obvious to your dad if you're faking it. But don't wait too long—delaying "I'm sorry" can cause further damage.

When I felt that I absolutely couldn't apologize to my dad's face, I wrote him an apology on a Post-it note. Most of the time, it wasn't more than "I'm sorry. I love you." It meant a lot to my dad, though. He still has those notes up in his office.

Also, remember the words of King Solomon, the wisest man who ever lived: "Kind words heal and help; cutting words wound and maim" (Proverbs 15:4 MSG). Next time you're tempted to launch a verbal assault at your dad, stop. Think. Then speak.

Relationship Lifters

- When you're tempted to tear into your dad, shut your mouth and put your arms around him. But be prepared to catch him when he faints. Those old guys can't take too much excitement.
- Next time you're in an argument with your dad, ask him if you can write him a letter instead. Don't have it out verbally; have it out on paper. But before you give it to him, read it! You'll probably want to tear it up. You might be able to give him the second or third letter. Make sure it's what you want to say. You can't erase hurtful words, but you can always rewrite a letter.
- Say you're sorry. We all make mistakes. I still get into arguments with my dad. I don't think I'd be breathing if I wasn't disagreeing with my dad. However, when you're wrong, admit it. Once again, be prepared to catch the old guy. And maybe dial 9-1-1.

Mom to Mom

Harsh words will pierce a mother's heart. We tend to either internalize the blows until they strip us of our dignity, or we externalize them so that the conversation quickly turns into a shouting match. Don't let yourself give in to either. The cost of bitterness and resentment in your relationship is too high. It will eat away your own soul. Fight it with God's power.

Distance your self-worth from your daughter's behavior. Just because she has chosen a path different from yours doesn't mean that you have failed as a mother. Don't let the enemy heap guilt and shame upon you, because it will not help you or her.

Continually pray for every person in your family. As you pray, focus on Christ rather than the situation. Praise Him that, although you can't see it now, you will trust Him to bring good and his glory out of your pain.

One specific bit of counsel our Christian psychologist gave me helped me deal with Heather's rebellion, even though at the time I didn't see its value. He said, "Relate to your own daughter as if she were your friend's daughter. That way everything is not so up-close-in-your-face personal." When I took his advice, it took off the edge of the intensity of the current situation and the verbal venom couldn't poison as deeply.

A Mother's Prayer

Help me remember the verbal scourging heaped on You during the last week of Your life. You didn't deserve any of it. Please give me Your heart of forgiveness and love that You displayed on the cross when You prayed, "Father, forgive them, for they know not what they do." Replace my stony heart with a new heart.

three

THE WAVE GOOD-BYE

*I am a child crying for mommy and daddy, lost in the desert,
and not hearing or seeing them. Please answer my cries. Pick me
up in your arms, like I was a baby, and carry me home. . . . I never
realized life could be so painful and lonely without people that you
love and that love you.*
—Entry in Heather Stone's Journal, March 12, 1996

For Dads

Painful emotions swirled through my mind during the fifty-minute drive from the hospital to the airport. With every glance at Heather in the rearview mirror, I wondered if I'd made the right decision. She was only thirteen.

Can I really send her to a desolate ranch in Utah? Will she come back changed? Should I pull off the next exit, turn around, and go back home? Perhaps she doesn't need something this severe. Then I reminded myself of the horror we had endured the past few months. Heather had left us no choice. She couldn't stay at our home any longer, at least for then. Even so, fear and guilt gnawed at my soul the closer we got to the airport.

I drove our Dodge minivan straight from the rehab facility. Our two other children sat in the far backseat. Heather and her mother sat in the center bench, away from the sliding door because we feared she might try to open it and bolt. As we passed the Hartsfield International Airport sign south of Atlanta, a dreadful thought surfaced: *Will she run from us once we step out of the car? Will she force me to physically carry her onto the plane?*

We pulled into the short-term parking and got out. So far so good. We nervously walked to the Delta check-in counter. As I placed the ticket on the counter, the chatty ticket agent glanced at Heather. "So, going to Utah, huh? Oh . . . you're going alone." She paused and then said, "It's beautiful out there. You'll really enjoy it."

I felt like bursting into tears and screaming, *This is no pleasure trip—we made this choice out of desperation. We did it only to keep our sanity.* Instead, I forced a plastic smile and mumbled a lie: "She's going to school out there."

After we reached the gate, Heather said she needed to use the bathroom. *Is this a ploy? Does she intend to run?* We agreed to let her go, if my wife escorted her and stood guard at the stall. I had to fight back tears as I watched Sherryl and Heather walk to the rest room. *Am I just a failure as a father? Has my failure culminated in this radical choice?*

I glanced at Tiffany, our youngest, only eight years old. She deeply loved Heather but also carried deep scars from the way Heather had treated her. Even so, her care package for Heather, a crumpled grocery bag filled with handpicked items, lay on her lap: A pack of Skittles. A coloring book with a dozen crayons rubber-banded together. Two old magazines. A small teddy bear. A sandwich bag stuffed with Fruit Loops. Several carefully folded notes, drawings, and pictures she had colored.

Then, as Heather and her mom walked back from the restroom, I saw her face in the full light. Our eyes locked. For the first time I clearly saw it: fear. Fear like that of a young doe frozen in the headlights of an oncoming car. Guilt overwhelmed me, and I had to look away to keep from sobbing in public.

Over the intercom came the announcement, "Now boarding flight 622 to Salt Lake City." We stood to help with Heather's carry-on and package from Tiffany. A few feet away from the boarding corridor we hugged, kissed, and cried. All but me. I didn't let myself cry because if I did, I'd lose it.

After Heather handed the agent her ticket, she slowly walked into the corridor. Then she stopped and turned toward us one last time. Tears welled up in her eyes. She feebly waved good-bye, turned, and disappeared into the plane. I'll never forget that final wave good-bye.

We stood at the floor-to-ceiling glass windows as her plane taxied down the runway and took off. Then, she was gone. We trudged back to our car. In silence we drove home as sadness weighed heavily on our hearts. We would not see our thirteen-year-old daughter for months. At the same time, we felt relief that we would enjoy peace at home for the first time in more than a year.

❈┉❈

What would lead a father to make such a torturous choice? What prompted me to send Heather to a desert in Utah? Dads, what should you look for that might force you to make such a choice? Perhaps my experience will give you clues to help determine if you must make a tough call.

For the previous several months, the tension snowballed in our home. Before we sent Heather to Utah, many people tried to help us avoid doing something like that. They included teachers, friends, school counselors, a lawyer, church leaders, the police, psychologists, psychiatrists, and a local treatment center for troubled teens.

Mom's Tip

Mom, the tough choices will likely tear your heart out. As best you can, remove your feelings from the decision. Consider how it could help your daughter and bring peace to your home.

During the months that led up to this crisis, we sought professional counseling from two different counselors. Both took strong Christian stands in their practice and came highly recommended. The first counselor didn't connect with Heather, and after a few meetings we realized we needed to change directions. The second counselor didn't connect with Heather the way she wanted him to. But we felt comfortable with him because his son had also rebelled. We believed his personal experience with his teen gave him credibility. We met with him weekly for several months, sometimes all of us, sometimes only Heather. His counsel helped us deal with the guilt that nagged us when we often wondered what we did wrong. He also gave Heather a sounding board to process her anger.

He referred us to a psychiatrist for further help. Based upon her recommendation, we admitted Heather to a local treatment center for difficult teens. They prescribed medication that seemed to take the edge off her explosive anger, and we hoped that the worst was over. It wasn't.

At the time she attended a legalistic Christian school that only complicated matters. When her rebellion became severe, the administrators expelled her. Although shocked, we understood their decision and enrolled her in another Christian school. When we met with the new principal, Heather tried to sabotage the interview by dressing in grungy clothes and green knee-high boots with heavy black eye shadow caked on her eyelids. With a letter of recommendation in hand from her counselor, I almost pleaded with the principal to give her a chance. We felt relieved when he said he'd try. However, five days later, the school expelled her because she brought Ritalin to school to snort and began to ask other students if they had drugs. She had stolen it from our medicine cabinet (one of our other kids had once had it prescribed). After this expulsion, tensions reached a boiling point.

Shortly thereafter, with fire in her eyes, Heather falsely threatened me as she growled, "I'm going to ruin you. I'm going to tell others that you've abused me." Were she to follow through on her accusation, she would jeopardize my career as a pastor and hurt our family. I immediately contacted our counselor and our lawyer just in case she made good on her threat.

When, a few days later, I told her that her actions might force us to place her in a boarding school, she threatened to take a gun and "put it to both of your heads and blow your brains out." Statements like this scared us, so we again admitted her to the treatment center for several days. After that stay, we enrolled her in an outpatient program that provided schooling and counseling during the day, but she spent her nights with us. Tensions subsided a bit during that time, and we hoped things would improve.

After Christmas we enrolled her in a public middle school. She had attended less than two months when I received an urgent call from the principal. With concern in her voice she said, "You must immediately come to the school. We found something in Heather's book bag, and we would not let her get on the bus."

My heart jumped, and I felt as if someone kicked me in the stomach. *Did she have a weapon? Had she bought drugs from someone? Did they find a note that accused me of abuse?*

I sped to the school and sprinted into the principal's office. I saw Heather slouched on the brown leatherette sofa just outside the principal's office. When she saw me, she looked away. The principal invited me to come into the office. I nervously took a seat as she handed me a crumpled note Heather had written. As I read it, my heart sank.

Laden with expletives, it detailed her plan to run away with friends. She wrote, "Let's go to Florida. Chuck's mom lives there and she'll let us stay without telling our parents. I hate this place. We could fly Value Jet. I'm going to steal some money from my parents."

With my head lowered, I trudged out of the office and drove her home in silence. That night we decided to readmit her to the center.

My wife and I stood at the door of her room as we explained our decision. The resulting explosion is forever etched into my mind. As soon as the words "We're taking you back to the hospital" came out of my mouth, she began to curse and scream, "I hate you! I'll never love you! I'm going to kill you!"

She then ran to her second-floor window and tried to jerk it open so she could jump out and run. I pried her away from the window and locked it as she dashed toward the door to escape. I ran to grab her and she yelled, "Don't rape me! I'm getting you for sexual assault. I'll ruin you. I hope you die!"

My wife called 911 on our cell phone as Heather cursed and struggled. She handed the phone to me, and I yelled to the operator, "Our daughter is going berserk. We're trying to take her to the hospital and she's fighting us. Please send the police—*now!*"

Heather grabbed a small knife from her desk. She waved it at us and said, "If you knew how much I hated you, I'd do it." Then she swung around, carved a crude pentagram on her wall, grabbed red nail polish, and painted it to resemble blood.

At that point we could do nothing but pray and hope the police arrived soon. That was actually the third call to the police in the last few months. For what seemed like an eternity, we stood at the door as she spewed expletives and threats. We feared she would turn the knife on us. A few minutes after the police arrived, they radioed for an ambulance. The paramedics strapped Heather onto a gurney and drove her to the local hospital.

After our nerves calmed, we drove to the hospital and learned that a sheriff was en route to take her to the center. I can still picture us standing in the hospital's emergency exit, waving good-bye to our thirteen-year-old daughter, who was being transported in the same sort of sheriff's van they used to carry criminals.

Two days later we put Heather on the plane to Utah.

For the next few days, both anguish and relief filled my heart. As I prayed, read the Bible, and tried to process the past few months, my thoughts often drifted to one of Jesus's most famous stories about a father's love. Jesus told a trilogy of stories in Luke 15 about finding lost things that depicted God's joy when someone comes to faith. The third story described a father's experience with his two sons often referred to as the parable of the prodigal son. Some scholars believe Jesus based this on a well-known true story.

The father in this account loved his sons and provided a good home for them. Yet, the younger one yearned for a life free from parental authority. His son wanted to get as far away from his father as he could, geographically and morally. He wanted to go to a "distant country" and live it up, as did Heather. And he didn't want to wait until his father's death to get his inheritance. One day he demanded his share. That was like telling his dad that he wished he were dead so that he could have his inheritance—his ticket to freedom—right then. (Jewish law did allow a father to give a son his inheritance before the father's death if he wanted to.)

Jesus didn't detail the father's response. But to make such a demand in that culture implied gross disregard for the feelings of a father, much like what we experienced with Heather. I imagine this request crushed the father's heart. He faced a tough decision. If he said no, his son might avoid the heartache the father knew awaited him. If he said yes, his son would experience many struggles, as Jesus described later in the story. Apparently the father took a few days to make his decision and convert property to cash. Perhaps he weighed the pros and cons. Maybe he consulted wise friends. I'm sure he prayed. He then made a tough decision (his "last straw") because this request probably had culminated years of his son's demanding attitude. He decided to give his son his inheritance. This would ultimately result in his son's misery, the natural consequences of his choice. Perhaps the father sensed that only through poor choices would his son turn around.

Dads, sometimes we also must make difficult choices that

bring pain to our daughters. Yet, because we love them as the prodigal son's father loved his son, we can't avoid those tough calls. In my case, I hoped that Heather's painful stay in Utah would bring her back to us and to God.

Mom's Tip

Mom, you and your husband must agree on your hard choices. As difficult as it seems, if you do agree, it will keep the decision from adding tension to your marriage.

As the writer of Hebrews wrote, "No discipline is enjoyable while it is happening—it is painful! But afterward there will be a quiet harvest of right living for those who are trained in this way" (Hebrews 12:11 NLT). In our case, after several years, this Scripture became a joyous reality for Heather. But, like the prodigal son's father, we didn't easily decide to send Heather away.

You may not face the situations the prodigal son's father experienced or the intense rebellion we faced with Heather. I hope you won't. But someday cir-cumstances may force you to make a tough decision for your daughter's sake. Consider these steps to guide your decision. They may bring you pain, take your time, and cost you money, but your daughter is worth it.

How to Apply Relational Life Preserver 3

1. Pray fervently before you make a final decision.

Before you make that tough call, make prayer a priority. God promises that he will give you wisdom. One of my favorite verses encouraged me through the decision-making process: "If you need wisdom—if you want to know what God wants you to do—ask him, and he will gladly tell you. He will not resent your asking" (James 1:5 NLT).

I used a simple reminder that helped me pray for Heather

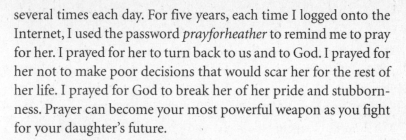
several times each day. For five years, each time I logged onto the Internet, I used the password *prayforheather* to remind me to pray for her. I prayed for her to turn back to us and to God. I prayed for her not to make poor decisions that would scar her for the rest of her life. I prayed for God to break her of her pride and stubbornness. Prayer can become your most powerful weapon as you fight for your daughter's future.

2. Determine whether your daughter is engaging in destructive behavior or simply making life difficult for you.

In chapter 1, I explained that we often panic when our daughters begin the inevitable transition into adolescence. We can't stop those changes, but we can help our daughters navigate them by refusing to panic. Make sure your relationship is really in the red zone. Destructive behaviors would include these:

- Drug and alcohol abuse.
- Attempting suicide.
- Running away or sneaking out at night to be with boys.
- Violence or threats of violence against others.
- Criminal behavior.
- Threats to accuse you of abuse or molestation.
- Refusing to attend school or repeated suspensions.

If these behaviors become routine or if you worry for her or your family's safety, you should take action.

3. Seek professional help.

Find a good Christian psychologist with whom both you and your daughter feel comfortable. We met several months with ours before we considered a program for Heather. He not only helped us deal with the family dynamics that contributed to her problems but also recommended a psychiatrist.

A good psychiatrist can help identify possible physiological problems. Sometimes mental illness lies at the root of our daughters' extreme rebellion. If ignored, the results can be dire, as Norm Wright illustrates:

> Of course, knowing how to handle an offending child is not easy. John Hinkley, for instance, who attempted to assassinate President Reagan, was a prodigal. His parents had tried various steps and treatments to help their drifting, failure-oriented child to attend school, work, live on his own and become self-sufficient. A psychologist advised them to use a "tough love" approach and turn him out of their home. But what this son needed rather than a tough love approach was hospitalization and treatment. He didn't need to be cut off from his parent's help. He was struggling with the distorted thinking pattern of schizophrenia, not willful disobedience. The story could have ended very differently had his parents discovered this earlier.[1]

This process may also reveal that your daughter has simply decided to rebel against you and your wife, and that the physiological dimension plays little part.

4. Consider the juvenile system.

When our crisis hit us, we were desperate. We searched for anything to give us relief and stop Heather's destructive behavior. Only after we sent her to Utah did we realize that our local county provided services for difficult teens. Our lawyer explained that parents could file charges against their children to seek the court's help.

Had we consulted our lawyer first, we probably would have taken this route before sending her to an outdoor program. Since her Utah experience did not solve all the problems, the following year we filed charges. As a result, the judge placed her on house arrest with an ankle monitor to alert the authorities if she ran away. He also assigned a probation officer to her whom she met with weekly. This relationship provided someone other than me and my wife to hold her accountable.

5. As a last resort, research and choose a facility in which to enroll her.

You may find a relative willing to take your daughter for a few weeks or months, but we didn't have that option. When we could no longer control Heather and saw where her destructive cycle was leading, I began to look for available options. With today's Internet, a simple search of phrases such as "wilderness therapy programs," "at-risk teens," or "residential treatment" will yield names of hundreds of options.[2] But when I was hunting, the Internet wasn't fully developed, so I relied on phone calls to a dozen programs I learned about from counselor referrals. After I received brochures, I chose to send her to Utah. In retrospect, however, I should have chosen a less-intense but longer program than the four-month-long one we chose.

Whichever you pick, choose wisely. Research it, ask for references, and visit it if possible.

6. Finally, maintain reasonable expectations about the program's success with your daughter.

Throughout Heather's stay, we monitored her progress through letters, reports from her caseworker, and a visit two months after she arrived. I unrealistically expected her to return "rehabilitated," back to her old compliant self. However, as soon as we drove out of the complex (we had gone to Utah to pick her up), she reverted to her old rebellious self. After we checked into the hotel, I even called the program directors and asked if they would take her back.

Back in Atlanta, though, we realized that the experience had had some effect. It took the hard edges off her attitude, at least for the time being, and she began to express appreciation to us more often. Our communication was more open and free because her stay had improved her self-image, giving her confidence in expressing her feelings honestly. Many battles remained, but her stay in Utah gave us a respite and slowed her destructive behavior.

If you must send your daughter away, keep expectations realistic. She probably won't return with all of her problems solved. But a good program can bring about positive change to improve your relationship.

Dads, tough calls will suck the life from you. But unless we make them, the relationships with our daughters may become irreparably damaged. The next chapter describes another painful choice dads must make, and perhaps the most critical one of all.

CHOOSING A PROGRAM FOR TROUBLED TEENS

Buddy Scott, an expert on troubled teens, recommends that a parent give attention to these factors before choosing a program.

- The leaders' beliefs.
- The leaders' concepts.

- The leaders' values.
- The leaders' programs.

- The leaders' attitudes.
- The leaders' competency.

- The leaders' love.
- The leaders' insightfulness.

- The leaders' approaches
- The leaders' spiritual maturity.[3]

Relationship Lifters

- Find a good time to talk to your daughter, and ask her what she thinks might happen if the relationship continues to deteriorate. Listen without giving your opinion. You want her to think about the possible consequences of her choices.
- Ask her what she thought about Heather's section of the book. If she hasn't read it, give her a bit of the background that led us to send her to an outdoor program and then ask her to read it. After she reads it, have the previous discussion again.
- Ask her to write down areas where you both could change to ease the tension. Develop a simple and workable plan to make those changes. Set a date to evaluate the plan's progress.

For Daughters

The song on the radio faded into static as we drove deeper into the wilderness. Then silence. Little did I know I wouldn't hear "real" music again for the next several months.

Dusk settled over the landscape as the old white Suburban rumbled along in rural Utah. The leather-faced cowboy driving and his wife in the passenger seat were silent, except for the crunch-crunching of the Corn Nuts they were eating. The front windows were cracked. The cold air felt like icy hands on my cheeks. I rubbed a hole in the fog of the side window and saw only the dark, ominous outline of the mountains against the nighttime sky and an endless sea of sagebrush. Like embers floating upward from a campfire, the first stars of the night began to peek out from the darkness. The moon cast a milky glow on the rocks and sand below. I sat back against the squeaky leather seat and tried to make myself comfortable as I leaned my head against the freezing window.

Though I refused to admit it, I was consumed with fear. I was alone in the middle of nowhere, at the mercy of strangers. I didn't know where they were taking me. And I'm sure I didn't want to go.

A few hours earlier they had "collected" me at the Salt Lake City airport. As I crept off the plane, I found it increasingly difficult to keep up my "tough girl" act. Anxiety and fear robbed me of my composure. Frantically, I tried to think of ways to escape but realized it was too late. Directly in front of me stood my "escorts." My fate was sealed.

Their appearance and solemn demeanor gave them away. Chuck, a red-haired cowboy with piercing blue eyes, a weather-beaten face, and a wiry red handlebar mustache, wore an old black Stetson, a faded flannel shirt, a belt buckle almost the size of a dinner plate, tight, creased Wranglers, and dusty black cowboy boots. He looked like someone straight out of a Clint Eastwood movie. His wife was a petite lady with short, frizzy blonde hair and glasses.

"You must be Heather," he said gruffly.

I glared at them and muttered, "Yes."

He curtly responded, "I'm Chuck. This is Connie. Let's go."

As we navigated our way through the crowded airport, I should have taken a better look at the sea of faces. That was my last sight of civilization for what seemed an eternity.

So there I sat in that old Suburban with cowboys I had never seen before while they drove me down the winding back roads of desolate Utah. I loathed the country—no malls or shows. I despised cowboys—too tight pants, too few teeth. I hated camping—bugs, dirt, and no showers. What would become of me at this terrible "ranch"? I would soon find out.

Only a few days earlier, I had called an inpatient rehab facility in Atlanta my temporary "home," though not for the first time. My counselors' and psychiatrists' concerns about my wild behavior led to the decision to send me to the ranch. It would take a lot more than a couple of weeks to "fix" me. They presented the idea of this slave ranch to my parents in a counseling session one day. Because of my actions (being expelled from school, sneaking out, making plans to run away, and so on), I left my parents with no other options. They sadly agreed with my counselors and decided to send me away.

"Hey, you! We're here!" the old cowboy barked. I groggily lifted my cold cheek off the freezing window. Slowly I took my things out of the vehicle and stepped out onto the dusty ground. My grungy jeans and flimsy T-shirt were useless against the icy wind.

We walked around to the front of the old, dark cabin. Dim lights in the windows cast a dull glow on the creaky porch. I could make out the edges of the worn logs, the splintered wooden pillars in front, and the old cattle dog sleeping in front of the door. It looked like a cabin straight out of a horror movie. I felt like an animal being led to the slaughter. I cautiously set foot inside the door. If fear had frozen me before, then it ate me alive. The front room contained nothing more than an old wood-burning stove, a few lanterns, and a rickety wooden table on the bare cement floor.

A stout, rugged woman with short, straw-colored hair and a weather-beaten face lumbered toward me like an angry pit bull. Her dark leathery skin was stark contrast to the icy green eyes that stared me down. She was deathly silent, except for raspy breathing. Then she abruptly ordered, "Give me your stuff! Now!" Except she didn't use a nice word like stuff. I had no choice. My father had signed temporary custody over to them. She owned me, and I had better obey.

She snatched my things from me and flung them on the table.

"Get that garbage off your face!" she said. I assumed she was referring to my heavy eye makeup. "We have no running water here. There's the wash basin." She pointed to a tin bowl of dirty water resting on the tree stump used as a makeshift stand. A sliver of gummy soap rested next to the sink. I hoped the freezing temperature of the water would wake me from my nightmare. However, that nightmare was my reality.

The next few months were some of the most difficult of my entire life. I was awakened daily at 5 a.m. to feed and water sheep in below-zero temperatures. We had to crack the four-inch layer of ice on top of the watering trough to pour the water in. I began to understand the concept of backbreaking manual labor.

After the morning chores of feeding the livestock, hauling firewood, and cooking and cleaning up after breakfast, I was turned over to a ranch hand for daily work projects. We dug fence posts in the hard, dry ground; built entire outbuildings and chicken coops; cleaned latrines, baled hay, hauled boulders; and cleaned manure out of livestock pens. My hands became tough and calloused, and I gained more than twenty pounds. I not only worked like a slave, but my freedom—that freedom I had fought so hard to attain when I was home—had vanished.

The place didn't allow makeup, haircuts, hair products, fingernail polish. They gave me only a toothbrush, toothpaste, Chapstick, and a plastic comb. Boyfriends and even boy and girl contact were out of the question. If I even mentioned relationships to any other resident, they made me sit in a dirt circle. I had to ask permission to use the latrine, to eat, to go outside, and even to speak. They told me what I could eat, when I could eat, and when I could sleep. They told me when (and if) I could bathe in the metal washtub. My only wardrobe choices were ratty T-shirts tucked into old jeans. There were no TVs, no CD or MP3 players, no computers, no cell phones. I was trapped in the middle of the Utah wilderness for four long months.

That horrible experience was my fault. I had made it impossible for my parents to control me. I was determined to do exactly what I wanted, when I wanted, where I wanted, and with whom I wanted. My parents were devastated.

At the age of thirteen, I began to smoke, drink, sneak out regularly, and mess around with boys—and my parents had no idea what to do. They felt their only option was to send me to the ranch. At the time, I hated them for it. I couldn't see past my own anger to recognize that my stay at the ranch was really the result of my actions. At the time I saw no value in this experience and still wonder how much it helped me. I do realize, however, that I forced my parents to make this drastic choice for my family's sake and to stop me from destroying myself.

So what's the point of my story? Don't push your parents to send you away. You *really* don't want to end up in the wilderness. I can't begin to describe the fear I lived with for those four months. I didn't know when I would get out . . . or if I ever would. At any given moment, they could command me to sit in a dirt circle for an indefinite amount of time and I couldn't say no. I had no say in my own life. It was imprisonment.

A famous Bible story in Luke 15 about a prodigal son is eerily similar to my experiences at the ranch. It tells about the son's desire for "freedom," the very thing I desired and lost. The prodigal son decided that he wanted to live "the good life." He demanded that his father give him his share of the inheritance early. Sadly, the father obliged. After only a short time of partying hard, the son saw his inheritance and his party friends disappear. His only option? Accepting a job as a caretaker of pigs. His new home was a foul-smelling, filthy pigsty.

I know all about pigsties . . . or maybe "cowsties." Have you ever shoveled through four feet of packed cow manure all day long? I did—and that was my prodigal pigsty. The prodigal son felt the weight of his actions when he slept in the mud and feces of swine. I felt the weight of my actions when I was alone among hundreds of smelly cows, shoveling their knee-high, slimy you-know-what.

Fortunately for the prodigal son—and for me—our fathers loved us enough to forgive us and receive us back with open arms. If you feel that you have strayed, don't let yourself reach the pigsty. Your reading this book is a step toward rebuilding that relationship with your father and avoiding what I experienced.

Consider these ideas to spare both you and your father the heartache of one of these places. Help him avoid making the *tough call* this chapter talks about.

- Is there something your dad asks you to do repeatedly, but you refuse to do it? Why don't you do it for once? It really won't hurt, unless he thinks you're trying to suck up to him to get away with something. Assure him you're not. It will make things a lot less painful.
- Do you *always* stay out past curfew? Do you stay on the phone long after you've been told to get off? Do you wear a short skirt or a skintight top that your father absolutely can't stand? Let him have his way this time. Come home early for once. Get off the phone. Change clothes. In addition to seeing his jaw drop (which can be quite funny), this simple act of obedience can greatly improve your relationship with your father.
- Do you do things that you know you shouldn't, such as drinking, smoking, or getting too physical with your boyfriend (just to name a few)? Ask yourself, "Why am I doing these things? How are they helping me?" Often, just thinking about your actions will help you realize what you already know.

- Are you doing anything so severe that it might force your dad to think about sending you to some place like the ranch? Rethink what you're doing! Do whatever is necessary to avoid a trip away. I guarantee that you have it better at home than you will at one of those places.

Relationship Lifters

- Compromise. Pick something you and your dad fight about a lot. Talk to him about it. Try to come to a compromise you can agree upon. (Getting along with your dad is much better than fighting with him!)
- Talk. Ask your dad if he's thought about sending you away. Ask him why. Find out what you can do to change, and do it! Stay at home! Avoid all forced camping experiences!

Mom to Mom

Precious mother, if you find yourself in a situation similar to Charles's and mine, the greatest advice I can give you is this: allow yourself to grieve. I felt a huge loss when Heather shattered my dream for a Christian home and refused to let me be the role model I wanted to be. My tears didn't take away the hurt, but they helped me process my pain.

Also, allow others into your life at this time. Let them know what you've experienced. If you keep it to yourself, they won't know you need help. When we returned home from the airport the day we sent Heather away, I couldn't make myself walk into her room. She left it a total wreck, and I couldn't bear the painful memories her room evoked. Two wonderful women from our neighborhood came over the next week, cleaned her room, and restored order to it again. Others sent me notes and cards. Many prayed for us. Let your friends nurture you.

Most importantly, don't shut God out. Satan will tempt you to blame the Lord for not intervening before the crisis. Your mind may tell you He's not to blame, but your battered emotions will cause you to feel that God let you down. When that happens, remember times when He proved His faithfulness to you. Cling to His Word. Meditate on this scripture God gave me in a desperate moment one morning during my quiet time.

"If you do not stand firm in your faith, you will not stand at all" (Isaiah 7:9).

A Mother's Prayer

*I praise You that You are a loving and
trustworthy God even when my emotions
and my circumstances suggest that You are
not. I release my daughter and
everything about her to You.
I humbly ask that You give me the faith
and the grace I need to stand on Your Word
and in Your character.*

four

WHEN LOVE LANGUISHED

Flood waters can't drown love,
torrents of rain can't put it out.
—Song of Solomon 8:7 (MSG)

For Dads

The smell of hot-dogs permeated the air. Other concessionaires sold Sweet Tarts and jumbo Snickers while I shoveled ice into white Styrofoam cups and poured soft drinks from two-liter bottles of Mr. Pibb. Every basketball parent took a turn at the hot-dog stand, and mine fell on that night. My son's team would soon play. It happened to be the big event of the season: Homecoming. And I was going to learn a painful lesson that night.

The agony began when the buzzer signaled halftime and the principal took the microphone. He called our attention to girls dressed in beautiful evening gowns. Arm in arm with each girl was a proud dad savoring the moment. Sadness and despair began to swell in my heart. My thoughts drifted to that moment years before when I first held Heather's tiny body. Gazing into her pink newborn face, I envisioned many happy experiences: bedtime stories, Christmas presents, visits to her grandparents. I never imagined I'd face the heartaches I was enduring.

A crew quickly set up a makeshift backdrop at center court.

Two fresh flower arrangements sat on white pedestals at each side. A teacher lined up the dad-and-daughter pairs directly in front of the concession stand. A hush fell over the crowd as music began. The principal then presented each girl. As he announced the girls' names, he described their accomplishments. Some volunteered at the local hospital. Others never missed a day of school. A few had earned high academic honors. He finished the introductions by reading each girl's favorite Bible verse.

As they took their places center court, the crowd cheered, leapt to its feet, and applauded. The girls smiled. The dads beamed. The moms cried. My spirit withered, and I wished I could crawl inside one of the cups. The contrast between Heather and those girls almost overwhelmed me. Anger boiled inside me. Instead of proudly showing off my daughter, I stood next to yellow ice coolers as my heart bled with humiliation about her downward spiral. Because of the pain caused by Heather's rebellion, my heart had grown cold toward her.

That night I felt physical pain when I tried to stifle my tears. A suffocating knot formed in my throat. My eyes burned as I forced myself not to blink. If I did, I knew the tears that pooled in my eyes would stream down my cheeks. I determined not to cry since real men don't cry (or so I thought). I rearranged my cups and shoveled ice to avoid the tears.

A sinister voice whispered to my soul, "Close your heart to her. She doesn't deserve your love. She hates you. Don't let her hurt you again. Let her go. Let her rebellion destroy her. Shut the door to your heart."

Everything inside me yearned to yield to that sinister voice and shut

Mom's Tip

Mom, if you sense your husband beginning to close his heart to your daughter, talk to him about your observation. Become his most fervent prayer partner as you pray for his heart to stay open.

Heather out of my heart. I felt no love for her, no fire to sustain the relationship, only coldness.

Then something happened. Another voice spoke to my soul, the kind voice of the Great Shepherd. He gently reminded me of his grace—his unmerited love for me and for her. He had never forsaken me, even at my worst. How could I forsake Heather?

At that moment, I chose not to extinguish my love for her. I allowed God's grace to prevail, and I left the door of my heart open to her. That decision would profoundly impact my relationship with Heather and affect her future.

Every father who experiences the extreme pain of a rebellious daughter will face a temptation similar to the one I faced: to close his heart to her, to quit loving. Fortunately, I made the right choice and later experienced the fruit of reconciliation. I faced many other temptations to close my heart to her, but that night became a defining moment in my love for her.

All prodigals don't return, but Heather did. In a beautiful letter she wrote years later, she described the love she felt from her mother and me during those times:

> Thank you for never closing your heart to me. I wouldn't be what I am now if you had. . . . I always felt the love of God from you . . . through your unrelenting pursuit of me in my times of darkness, through never giving up on me, through everything you did for me in spite of how horrible I was. . . . That's how God loves us.

The experiences of the biblical character Joseph describe how he had every reason to close his heart to his brothers. Because his father "loved Joseph more than any of his other sons" (Genesis 37:3), his brothers began to resent him. After seventeen years of his favoritism, their anger toward Joseph culminated one day in a conspiracy to kill him. Fortunately, the oldest brother, Reuben, convinced them to spare his life. They threw Joseph into an empty well and later sold him to a caravan of slave traders. The chain of events these actions set in motion certainly would push most people to close their hearts towards those who had caused such pain. But not Joseph.

He ended up as the slave of Potiphar, one of the Egyptian pharoah's officials. God blessed him, though, and he rose to a place of prominence in this official's household. Then Potiphar's wife falsely accused him of rape. He got tossed into another hole, this time a prison. But God blessed him again, and the warden of the prison placed the entire prison under Joseph's care. Joseph's get-out-of-jail card finally came when he interpreted one of Pharoah's dreams. As a result, Pharoah placed Joseph in charge of a program to store up grain to prepare for a coming famine that would affect the entire region.

One day Joseph's brothers showed up to ask for grain. They didn't recognize him, but he recognized them. That was his opportunity to take revenge. After all, their decision twenty years prior led to rejection, abandonment, loss of family, slavery, imprisonment, and false accusations. Although Joseph certainly struggled with his feelings toward his brothers, he kept his heart open to them. When he revealed his identity, they reacted with fear because they knew Joseph had the power to have them killed. But with tears he embraced his brothers, extended forgiveness, and met their needs.

Although his brothers gave him every reason to close his heart to them, Joseph chose not to. Heather's choices never caused me the terrible problems Joseph faced. Her rebellion did, however, bring heartache, shame, and disappointment.

Dads, have issues with your daughters thrown you into a pit of anger and disappointment? Have you felt the sting of rejection, the heaviness of sorrow, and the embarrassment of shame? Joseph's example teaches us that by God's grace, we can keep our hearts open to our rebellious daughters if we consciously try to keep the love alive.

How to Apply Relational Life Preserver 4

When my son, Josh, and I camp, we always make a campfire. At night, before we climb into our sleeping bags, we usually let it die all the way down. The next morning we stoke the fire with a stick to find any remaining hot embers to reignite it. Likewise, when love for our daughters begins to die down, we dads must look for ways to stoke the relationship fire to reignite it. Consider these ways to keep your love for her alive.

1. Prepare yourself for circumstances that will tempt you to quit loving.

Perhaps you've not yet experienced a situation so painful that it snuffs out your love for your defiant daughter. If not, you likely will at some point. One mother described her reaction to notes she discovered that vividly described her daughter's sexual experiences. As she sat on her bed and read her daughter's words, her "universe turned slowly upside down . . . [and] rage of a kind she had never before experienced, a blind and murderous rage that shocked her even more than the letters she had read, left her frightened, breathless, weak."[1]

During the most intense times in our relationship, Heather said or did things that nearly overwhelmed me with rage. She screamed, insulted, and cursed me. She verbalized that she hated me, our family, and God. She then did something spiteful to prove her point.

I often felt tempted to say, "Okay, fine. You hate me. You hate our family. Then get out. I don't want you here. I don't want to see your face. I hate you, too!" When she was fourteen I kicked her out of our home. But the next day, as I sat in the principal's office with three school officials, they informed me that legally I couldn't do that. (So much for tough love.)

Although occasionally I said hateful words in response to her hate, usually I took Buddy Scott's counsel when he wrote, "Don't make relationship-ending remarks like: 'I never want to see you again; If you step out that door, it's over with us forever; Go ahead and kill yourself, and see if I lose any sleep over it!'"[2] He reminds us what Paul wrote in Romans 12:21 (CEV), "Don't let evil defeat you, but defeat evil with good." Had I verbalized my lack of feelings of love for Heather and closed the door of my heart forever, the relationship would have died.

Your daughter is growing up, and you're trying to figure out how to let her grow up. Guard against universal edicts. Don't say what you feel like saying. If you can't love her with your emotions, love her with your mind. Tell yourself, "Right now, I feel no love for my daughter, only anger, rage, and disgust. But by God's grace, I will choose to love her, regardless of my feelings."

2. Deal with your anger.

God gave us anger as a normal human emotion. We don't sin each time we feel or express anger; however, anger left to fester can burrow inward and become bitterness. The writer of Hebrews warned, "Make sure that no one misses out on God's wonderful kindness. Don't let anyone become bitter and cause trouble for the rest of you" (Hebrews 12:15 CEV). Anger can also explode outward and devastate our daughters with its poison (see chapter 2).

> *Mom's Tip*
>
> Mom, you, too, will experience the temptation to close your heart to your daughter. If you begin to feel that way, bring another woman you trust into your life. Share your feelings with her.

Max Lucado cautions us to deal with our anger before it becomes destructive to us and to others:

> Resentment is the cocaine of emotions. . . . It causes blood to pump and energy level to rise. It demands increasingly larger and more frequent doses. There is a danger point at which anger ceases to be an emotion and becomes a driving force . . . and like cocaine anger kills . . . physically, emotionally, and spiritually . . . it shrinks the soul.[3]

We must make the right choice in response to our anger. We can bury it and let it turn into bitterness. We can blame others. I did. When Heather began her downhill slide, I looked for someone on which to cast blame: her friends, school, the church youth group, MTV, too much Mountain Dew, Care Bears, anything that might have contributed to her rebellion. I came to realize that ultimately she chose to rebel. Neither of these two choices helps us deal with our anger. The only right choice is to process it in a God-honoring way. Consider these simple steps the next time you feel anger toward your daughter.

- Express your feelings. Make a list of everything that makes you feel angry. Share your feelings with someone you trust. Determine whether you should or shouldn't share those angry feelings with your daughter. Doing so may or may not help, so use discernment.
- Release your feelings through a physical activity (such as sports or lawn work).
- Confess to God your inadequacy to deal with your daughter.
- Change how you previously expressed your anger toward her.
- Release any resentment you feel toward your daughter.[4]

Don't let your anger rise to the point that one parent realized: "I know now that when they turned their backs on me they were running away from my anger."[5]

3. Don't go it alone. Ask family and friends to help.

When Heather began to rebel, we felt alone and isolated. We battled feelings of guilt and wondered what others would think of our failed parenting. As a pastor I struggled with what others would think about my leadership. Fortunately, we included others in our support network.

One couple rode with us on one trip to a treatment center. Our church leadership gave me time off when we flew to other parts of the country to visit Heather in the treatment programs. Our own parents encouraged us throughout the difficulties. One woman in our church often prayed for Heather and became her sounding board.

> **Starting a Support Group**
>
> Teen counselor Buddy Scott's book *Relief for Hurting Parents* provides excellent suggestions for starting a support group for hurting parents. Check out www.buddyscott.com for more information and resources on how to start a group.

Sometimes, however, you may receive unsolicited advice and spiritual platitudes. Don't let that possibility hinder you from confiding in others who will support you. Sharing struggles does not make you less of a parent. As Proverbs 24:6 (CEV) states, "Battles are won by listening to advice."

A letter that describes your situation and asks for prayers provides a good way to include others. But as you consider with whom to share your struggle, choose those who . . .

- will accept your feelings and keep your confidences.
- won't give unhelpful advice or spiritual clichés.

- believe you can make it through this tough time.
- won't pull away because of your tears and your anger.
- have experienced their own personal pain.
- will keep their promises to you.
- will really pray for and with you.

4. Find a catalyst to stoke the relationship fire that reaches the depths of your heart.

Many men struggle to express emotions such as sadness and tenderness. We tend to operate more from our minds than our hearts. But our daughters need to sense that we connect with them at a heart level. The feeling we must convey to our daughters is embodied in the definition of the Hebrew word *racham,* which is translated "compassion." It means "to soothe, cherish, and love deeply like parents." It's the kind of feeling babies evoke. This type of emotion can help our daughters feel our love and care.

John Eldredge notes, "Emotions are the voice of the heart. . . . They express the deeper movements of the heart."[6] He expands on this idea:

> The heart lives in the . . . bloody and magnificent realities of living and dying and loving and hating. That's why those who live from their minds are detached from life. Things don't seem to touch them very much; they puzzle at the way others are so affected by life, and they conclude others are emotional and unstable. Meanwhile, those who live from the heart find those who live from the mind . . . unavailable. . . . That is . . . the number one disappointment of children who feel entirely missed or misunderstood by their parents.[7]

As I said, relentless rebellion from your daughter will tempt you to close your heart toward her and relate to her only from your mind or with anger. Heather's rebellion often did that for me. God knew I needed something that would pry open the door of my heart. I needed to know that I still loved Heather. It happened one Tuesday morning.

Three years into Heather's rebellion, our struggles continued to mount. I was fed up with her antics, and she had exhausted my patience. My anger teetered on the edge of rage. I wondered if I could possibly love her again.

I kept an office in the basement of our home and studied there in the mornings before I went to the church office. One December morning, after another weekend of turmoil, I forced myself to go downstairs. I sat down, flipped on my computer monitor, and stuck a Christmas CD in the CD player. I began to try to work.

"It's the most wonderful time of the year . . ." sounded from the speakers.

That's a bunch of bunk. Not for me this year. It's more like the worst time of the year, I thought.

". . . And everyone telling you, 'be of good cheer' . . ."

Sure, as if I can be of good cheer with a daughter like Heather.

". . . It's the hap-happiest season of all . . ."

Maybe if you don't have a teenage daughter bent on destroying your family, it could be.

". . . There'll be much mistletoe-ing and hearts will be glowing when loved ones are near . . ."[8]

My mind exploded. *I don't want Heather near me! I can't call her a loved one. I feel no love for her right now. I may never. My infuriation at her overwhelms any scant feelings of love. I can't allow her to hurt me anymore. No . . . I won't let her hurt me anymore!*

God, I will soon close my heart to her. The door barely remains ajar now. One more hurt from her, it shuts . . . forever. When it does, I will never open it to her again. Never.

"Enough of that music," I said out loud. I mouse-clicked to the next song.

Then, as if Jesus grabbed me by the shoulders and shook me,

the next track arrested my attention. It began with chirping of crickets and other nature sounds followed by gentle ringing of Christmas bells. Then ... "Silent night, holy night, all is calm, all is bright. ..." A mellow violin resonated with bells ... then a gentle blowing breeze ... and more warm violins. Something began to happen to my heart. Heat rose behind my eyes and I felt a sting. Tears flooded my eyes. I began to weep. Sobs racked my body. Hot tears flowed down my cheeks.

Being reminded of that majestic moment when divinity intersected with humanity in the birth of Jesus, my emotions overwhelmed me. These thoughts came to my mind: *Lord, You came with an open heart you knew I would break. You knew I would reject and hurt you often. Yet, your love for me never wavers. You've never closed your heart to me. How can I close my heart to Heather? Who am I to reject her?*

Just then I heard footsteps on the stairs. I tried to wipe my tears away. The door creaked on its hinges and opened. I couldn't believe who stood there: Heather. I turned my head away but it was too late. She had already seen my red eyes. She walked around my desk and stood behind me. She wrapped her arms around my chest and laid her head on mine. Hot tears again flooded my eyes and dripped onto her slender white arms.

Then I felt warm drops of moisture on my head. *Were they Heather's tears?* Yes. Somehow her tears became ointment to my wounded heart. As our two sorrows inter-mingled, I knew that my heart would always stay open to her.

"Silent Night" ended, and I hit "Play" again. I wanted to relish this holy moment. When the violins finished Heather unwrapped her arms that now glistened with tears. She quietly began to leave and to close the door. I then told her what I'd strained to tell her the past three years. I could then say it with renewed commitment. "I love you, Heather."

The next day I settled into my familiar gray swivel chair for another day's work. I noticed something on my computer monitor. A slightly smudged orange Post-it note with Heather's distinctive handwriting read, "I love you, too, Dad."

Love, which lay in ashes one day prior, had risen like the Phoenix, reignited with new hope. Now, years later, when I sit in that same well-worn gray swivel chair, many smudged Post-its with "I love you" that I've taped to my desk remind me of that defining moment in my life when I learned never to close my heart to love.

Something mysterious and supernatural happened that morning. Where words had failed to communicate love, those tears spoke with clarity. Although our troubles would continue and anger would still surface, I knew God had opened the door of my heart to Heather—permanently. A bonding occurred upon which God continues to build upon to this day. God allowed us to experience what King David wrote in Psalm 30:5 (NASB): "Weeping may last for the night, but a shout of joy comes in the morning."

Pray that God will bring emotional catalysts into your life to stir the remaining embers of love. Look for them. Stay open to them because they may come when you least expect them. As Eldredge wrote, "a fragrance in the air, a certain passage of a song, an old photograph falling out from the pages of a book, the sound of somebody's voice in the hall . . . [can make] your heart leap and [fill] your eyes with tears."[9]

Although the following options may sound odd, you'll be amazed how they can evoke emotion. For example, as I wrote this chapter I was listening to a classical Internet radio station. Every year I take our youngest daughter to see *The Nutcracker*. The Internet station began to play selections from that ballet, unexpectedly stoking warm thoughts about Tiffany. Consider these catalysts to stoke your love toward your daughter.

- Listen to music your daughter enjoyed when she was younger.

- Read again a storybook you read to her when she used to sit in your lap.
- Hold your daughter's favorite teddy bear.
- Look at her baby book or scrapbooks your wife made for her.
- Find some Father's Day cards she made for you when she was younger.
- Look at pictures or home videos of fun times you experienced with her.
- Find her baby clothes and, as you hold them, remind yourself of the tenderness you felt toward her then.
- If she has a favorite music box, wind it up and listen to it.
- Smell baby powder to evoke images and feelings when you held her as an infant.
- Visit a place that brings back good memories.

I know you may feel awkward doing these things, but they carry great power to soften our hearts and remind us how much we love our girls. Don't succumb to the temptation to close your heart to your daughter. Don't write her out of your life. Don't lose hope. Keep the flame lit so that your daughter can feel in her heart what the prodigal son felt. Even though the prodigal ran away and didn't deserve to return, he knew deep inside that his loving father would receive him if he ever came home again.

RELATIONSHIP LIFTERS

- What catalytic experience do you believe could stoke your love for your daughter? When will you do it?
- Ask your daughter what special memories stand out about your relationship with her. Ask her why they stand out. Communicate to her that you'd love to create new special memories.

- If you've not yet been tempted to close your heart to your daughter, write down what you will do should her rebellion tempt you to shut her out.
- Consider allowing your daughter to see you cry tears of love for her. Ask God to create catalytic situations when you both are together.
- Ask your daughter for suggestions on how she'd like you to change your angry responses to her when she blows it.

For Daughters

I can't do it.

I slumped back in the dirt—alone, frightened, on the verge of tears, and utterly defeated. I stared blankly at the sagebrush-spotted mountains surrounding me. The spindle and the ember board lay where I'd left them. The bow lay where I'd flung it. My back ached from hunching over, my head pounded, my knees were swollen and stiff from kneeling, and my hands felt arthritic. *Why do I have to do this? Why? Why?* I hung my head between my knees and began to sob.

As you've learned in earlier chapters, when I was thirteen years old, my parents sent me to a work ranch in Utah for "wayward kids" (in my case, a serious understatement). The entire program was nothing like the hospital-type environments I'd encountered before. The program's purpose was to show us how much we took for granted. They used these backwoods tasks and backbreaking labor not only to exhaust us physically, but also to break us down mentally and emotionally.

Bow-drills. My own personal curse word. What were these wretched bow-drills? Sane, well-adjusted people prefer the usual method of lighting a fire (such as matches or lighters). Not at this ranch. The method they forced me to use was the bow and drill method. It involves using sticks and rocks to start a fire. What would possess anyone to use this method still lies beyond my comprehension, but these sadistic (that's how I saw them) cowfolk believed that we (meaning us wayward kids) needed it.

So, to make an ember (a smoldering bit of burning wood), I took the small ember board and placed the larger fireboard on top of it so they made a *T* shape. Carved notches along the edge of the fireboard caused the punk (the smoking beginnings of the ember) to fall on the ember board. But this was only the first step.

I then held the spindle, rock, and bow. The spindle is a piece of wood stripped of its bark that resembles a thick pencil, with one end sharpened to a point. The bow is made from a bent stick with nylon rope tied to both ends. (It resembles an Indian bow.) The flat, smooth rock has a tiny notch carved in one side.

Oh, but this is only the set-up. To create this insidious ember, I needed to step on the fireboard, kneel on the ground with my left knee, loop the bowstring around the spindle, insert the point of the spindle into the notch carved at the edge of the board, press down on the spindle with the rock, and whip the bow back and forth with as much pressure and speed as I could muster.

It's not really necessary to understand what I'm describing. (Just remember: *never* ask for a "primitive firemaking" set for Christmas. They do exist; my dad downloaded an order form.) I didn't think it was funny. Rather, realize that it's one of the most terrible and frustrating tasks ever invented by humanity, much like anything involving logarithms and square roots—and much like getting along with your dad.

To see one of these fire-starting weirdo cowboys make an ember, you'd think it was easy. But ha! Not for anyone who wasn't raised by wolves. I slaved over the stick and bow for eight days, and I made only one ember, and that only because I got lucky. So I was banished to a dirt circle until the task was complete. I had lost all hope. I was barely a teenager, twenty-five hundred miles from home, at a dilapidated cabin with no electricity or running water. They didn't allow me to bathe for seven days, and I changed clothes only once. I wasn't allowed to speak unless spoken to. The only thing I could do without asking—I couldn't sleep, read, or talk unless they gave me permission—was bow-drills.

So there I was, staring hopelessly at the spindle at my knee and the bow lying in the dirt behind me. *This is ridiculous. I shouldn't be here. I've done nothing to deserve a punishment like this. Who sent me here?* I angrily narrowed my eyes and clenched my fists. *Dad! This is all his fault. If he really loved me, he wouldn't have sent me here. I hate that man....*

Finishing a bow-drill was one of the hardest things I've ever done in my life. Exerting force and pressure long enough to create an ember took its toll physically, emotionally, and mentally. But if I did finish it, it would be more than worth it: I'd get to *the barn.*

I know that doesn't sound like much, and it wasn't. But for me, who called a thin piece of foam "bed," the creek "the washing machine," a tin washtub "the bath," and an outhouse "the rest room," the barn was the Ritz Carlton. At the barn I gained some freedom. It had water faucets and showers that I could use every other day. Instead of gas lamps, there were light switches. I would get a mattress and even a pillow. The laundry lady washed clothes, so no more hand-laundering in the creek. In short, it gave me the essentials I had grown to depend on in my thirteen years. By no means was the barn luxurious, but it meant no more dirt circle and no more bow-drills. And it meant I was closer to returning home.

So I was determined not to let some sticks and a rock defeat me. I wanted something, anything, better than my life then. Sometimes your relationship with your dad can feel as if you're making a fire with a bow and drill. They're both hard work. They both can get old very quickly. Physically, mentally, and emotionally, they're exhausting. And, at times, they both seem hopeless and a waste of time. But just as completing the bow-drills ultimately granted me a spot at the barn, building and repairing your relationship with Dad will bring you rewards. Tension between the two of you can subside. Fights can become fewer. Anger will lessen. Life will get easier.

When I took my first shower at the barn (the best in my entire life), had my first night's sleep there and my first change of clothes in over a week, I realized that my persistence was worth the effort. If you stick it out with your dad and refuse to close your heart to him, you will reap the rewards of your hard work.

Think about it. What Bible character perfectly exemplified love? Who was betrayed, denied, and abandoned in his greatest time of need—all by his best friends? Who was mocked, beaten, and nailed to a cross by those he was giving his life for? Who kept his heart open to those who hurt him the most? And who set aside bitterness and anger and chose unconditional love? Jesus. Though we break his law every day, he chooses to love us. Though we defy him when we ignore what he asks of us, he chooses love. Though we betray him, deny him, and abandon him, he greets us with open arms every time we return to him.

In his own human way, my dad wanted to love me as Jesus loves me. Maybe your dad desires the same for you. But we've got to help our dads. What's one of the best ways to do that? Don't shut your dad out of your life. Take advantage of this wonderful gift that God has given you (and that many others wish they had)—a father.

I wish I had taken my own advice growing up. Sadly, I did not. For years, I shut my dad out of my life and heart. I kept Dad as far from me as I could and deemed him Public Enemy #1. I disrespected and deceived him. I channeled all my bitterness at him. I took out all my anger on him. I don't know why I did this, but I do know that I regret it deeply.

Don't miss out on your dad! Consider these ways to avoid my mistakes and to help your relationship with your dad thrive.

Be ready.

Prepare for the times when you'll want to shut him out. For me those times occurred whenever my dad did anything I didn't agree with—meaning almost all the time. If he told me not to use the phone after eleven, I hung up at one. When he discovered me sneaking out at night, I resented him for catching me. When he bought me a present "just because," I rolled my eyes. When he told me he loved me, I ignored him and walked away.

Don't make the same mistakes I did. Identify what makes you want to keep your dad out of your life, and fight it. Avoid universal statements that put up walls, such as, "I'm never talking to you again," or "You'll never change," or "You always ..." In a fit of rage, it's easy to say or think these things. Force yourself not to.

Realize your dad may feel the same way you do.

Do you ever feel that your dad is trying to make life more difficult—that he destroys your plans and ruins your fun? Think about it—what are you doing to him? Are you making it easy for him to be a father? Are you cooperating with him? Are you making his rules necessary? As much as you may feel that he's a constant interruption in your life, it goes both ways!

My dad sacrificed many nights of sleep waiting up for me. He took weeks off work to fly out to the various treatment centers where I stayed. He spent hours of his free time researching treatment programs for troubled teens and spent tens of thousands of dollars of his own money putting me in those places. He drove me to and from my probation officer meetings. He found my cigarettes and threw them away. He grounded me when I came home drunk. He kicked boys out of the house. But all these things he did were exclusively for my benefit—not his own.

How did sneaking out benefit me? How did drugs and alcohol help me? Did my expulsions from school "build me a better tomorrow"? No! So put yourself in your dad's shoes. He probably struggles with the same feelings of hopelessness, anger, and frustration in your relationship that you do. Look at your relationship through his eyes, and maybe you'll see things differently. Perhaps you'll understand the way he feels, and therefore, the way he acts . . . and this can benefit you both.

Talk about your feelings.

I can't overstate this one. When you and your dad have a blowout fight, don't allow your anger and bitterness to fester.

A brown recluse spider bit a friend of mine who didn't realize it until it was almost too late. The bitten area on her leg started to ooze, and the skin around it turned black. The poison literally ate a hole in her leg. A deep scar on the side of her calf reminds her of that bite.

This can happen to your heart if you're not careful. Don't allow the poison of bitterness to begin to kill parts of your heart. Don't ignore the "wound" that a problem with your father can cause. It can fester into bitterness. Deal with the problem before permanent relational damage sets in. Talk it out with your dad or with someone objective who can help you deal with your frustration.

Avoid regrets.

Don't make the same mistakes I made. Thankfully, my dad and I have an amazing relationship today. He helps me in every part of my life: job applications, college, planning, financially, and with boys. He encourages me, supports me, and helps me in any way he can. And he changes my windshield wipers, as that's the extent of his fix-it capabilities.

Our current relationship was incomprehensible only a few years ago. I could have enjoyed these benefits all through my teenage years, but instead I chose to sabotage our relationship with what I did. Don't let your actions destroy a good thing. Your dad can be your greatest ally; don't deny him that opportunity. Back then I thought I didn't need his help. How wrong I was. My dad is now one of my best friends. I'm serious—I am not being paid to say this. Your dad can be one of your best friends too. Don't choose to destroy your relationship with your dad by doing things that push him away. Leave your heart open to him.

Just as bow drills seemed a ridiculous, time-consuming, and unproductive thorn in my side, so might getting along with your dad. If you disagree and constantly fight, take the time and effort to work out your differences. It will take patience, but I assure you—it's worth it! When I finished the bow drills, they brought me the rewards of the barn. If you keep things right with your dad, you will experience the joy of a solid relationship. The end result? Much more than hot showers and a better mattress. You'll enjoy a lasting, special relationship that will grow and endure through the years. I assure you—*it's worth it.*

dads gone CRAZY

Relationship Lifters

- This week, look at old pictures or at the gifts he's given you over the years. Don't be blinded by the present pain and conflict; look back to the past to relive the better times.
- Check yourself. Each time you want to direct your anger toward your dad, stop and think. Are you angry at him? Or are you angry that he caught you breaking the rules, that you're fighting with your best friend, or that you can't do what you want? Figure out the source of your anger. Don't make Dad the punching bag.
- Write a letter to your dad this week. Written words can be better than spoken ones—you can rewrite, throw away, and modify letters; but you can't erase what you speak. Tell him that you want to keep him in your life, but that It's hard. And tell him why. He may be clueless. Use "I" statements in your letter, and take responsibility for your wrong actions. Don't place all the blame on him.

Mom to Mom

We once owned a crazy dog we named Joey. When someone came to our door, he barked incessantly and disregarded all our commands. As an act of desperation, we enrolled him in obedience school at a local pet store. They required one of us to attend each class with him. He amazed us as he vacillated between aggression, compliance, and wild-eyed panic at each class. When the six-week class concluded, the trainer insightfully commented, "I've seen animals like this many times before. They are known as *fear biters.*"

As I thought about that term, it made a lot of sense. Some animals snap, bite, and act out because of a deep root of inner fear. Teenagers can also act that way. Deep emotional stresses often give way to out-of-control, roller-coaster behavior.

When your daughter acts in such unreasonable ways that they dash hope, look beyond the surface to her inner world. Ask yourself, "What thoughts and emotions fuel her rebellious behaviors?" Ask the Lord to give you wisdom to discern the needs of your daughter's heart. Consider these scriptures as you work to understand your daughter's inner world.

"The words of a man's mouth are deep waters, but the fountain of wisdom is a bubbling brook" (Proverbs 18:4 NIV).

"The purposes of a man's heart are deep waters. But a man of understanding draws them out" (Proverbs 20:5 NIV).

A Mother's Prayer

*O Lord, only You truly know my
daughter's heart. Give me understanding
to look past her surface behaviors
to discover how I can touch
the deepest needs of her heart.
Give me the wisdom to reach her
on the level in which she needs ministry.
I fully commit her into Your hands.*

five

THE HALLMARK MOMENTS

Most of all, love each other as if your life depended on it.
Love makes up for practically anything.
—1 Peter 4:8 (MSG)

For Dads

Our troubles with Heather continued to mount. As a result, we faced another trip to a different treatment program, this time to blustery Boston in the dead of winter. As finances were tight, my wife and I decided that to save money I'd take her to Boston by myself.

A few days later, we arrived on a cold, cloudy day. After I rented a car and marked my map, we drove straight to the psychiatric hospital. The entrance to this unit was on the side of the hospital, perhaps to minimize the stigma embarrassed parents felt about bringing their children there. After we signed in, I filled out the paperwork as a nurse escorted Heather down the sterile corridor. Once more, I waved good-bye to my daughter and hoped that this stay would help her. My plane didn't leave for two days, so I planned to visit her the next day.

I checked into an inexpensive motel and asked the clerk about the nearest restaurant. She gave me directions to a nearby buffet (my favorite kind). I took the poorly lighted stairs to the second floor, found my room, and tossed my small suitcase on the tattered bedspread. I then bundled up to face the brisk wind and drove to the buffet. The food seemed hard to swallow as I mulled over Heather's problems.

I finished dessert, a soft-serve ice cream cone that I wished I could have shared with her. With time to kill, I paid my tab and I walked across the street to a gift shop.

Meandering through the store, I noticed a display of music boxes halfway down one aisle. High-intensity lamps aimed at the display created a surrealistic feel, as if the boxes beckoned me to play their music. I picked up several and turned them over to see the price. I thought, *Ouch! Expensive.* For some reason, one box stirred my curiosity, so I flipped it over and wound the brass key to see what it would play. The nostalgic music caught me off guard. I didn't expect that song, nor was I prepared for the emotions it evoked.

Six decades ago Judy Garland captured the hearts of America when she played Dorothy in the movie *The Wizard of Oz.* I saw the movie on TV as a seven-year-old and hadn't given it much thought since then. But, as the music box played her most famous song, "Somewhere Over the Rainbow," I actually recalled most of the lyrics. As I thought of Dorothy's hope that blue skies lay beyond the rainbow and that her dreams could come true, uncertainty flooded my heart. *Will my dreams for Heather come true? Can blue skies replace the dreariness in our relationship?*

I hurried to the other end of the store to hide behind the card racks just in case I cried. Then, a thought struck me: *Buy a gift for Heather. She certainly doesn't deserve it. But show her that you love her anyway.*

I sensed the impression came from God, so I decided to act on it. As I scanned the card rack, I saw the perfect card—the largest one in the entire store. Unopened, it measured almost two feet high and one foot wide. On the front a contented Chihuahua with a wistful look stood with his feet in a pair of tennis shoes almost as large as he. With his head cocked he seemed to look right at me. Because Heather had often said that she wanted a Chihuahua, I thought this might encourage her. (A few years later Peanut, a chubby brown Chihuahua, became part of our household as Heather's dog.)

After buying it, I noticed I felt less discouraged. Somehow, the small act of buying a "grace gift" for someone who didn't deserve it brought hope to my heart.

The next day I woke early to arrive at the unit when visiting hours began. I found the pediatric wing on the third floor, went through the security door at the end of the hall, and pushed the intercom button to let the staff know I wanted to visit Heather. The nurse buzzed open the locked door. As I walked down the drab hallway, she told me where I could find her.

When I reached Heather's room, I set the card against the outside wall and lightly tapped on her door. When she didn't answer, I slowly opened it and saw her sitting on the bed. We chatted a bit. I could tell that she was scared. I said, "I got you something. I hope you like it."

As I pulled out the card from the white bag I'd carried it in and gave it to her, I said, "I love you." The card read, "Hurry and get well. . . ." (And inside:) "No one else could fill your shoes!" I signed it "Love, Dad."

I didn't realize the significance of that gift (and others like it) until years later. Several times during the lowest points of our relationship, I gave Heather similar grace gifts when she least deserved them: a special ring for her sixteenth birthday when a few days earlier she had spent the whole night out and lied about it, a butterfly mobile during a family trip she had ruined, a yellow rose when she was most demanding.

Grace gifts to Heather communicated my love to her more than words ever could. Not only did they soften her defensive barriers, but they helped me as well. When I gave to her unconditionally, God infused hope into my heart. These undeserved gifts that injected life into our relationship created what I call "Hallmark moments"— mo-ments much like Hallmark's Christmas commercials that convey hope, love, and warm memories.

The Bible recorded one of the world's greatest Hallmark moments when the prodigal son's father responded to his son's return.

Mom's Tip

Mom, you, too, can communicate God's grace to your daughter through simple gifts. Consider what you could give to communicate your unconditional love for her.

The Bible doesn't say how long the father waited, prayed, and yearned to see his wayward son again. But it does say that his dream became a reality. Scripture implies that he scanned the horizon daily to look for his son. One day the father noticed a speck that moved in the distance. As he squinted and the speck grew, he realized it was someone walking toward him. As the person got closer, his gait seemed familiar. Could it be who he hoped it would be? Could it? As his eyes focused, he then realized that familiar walk was indeed his son's. He ignored the pain of an old man's legs and with joy ran to his son to shower him with kisses.

At that point the father had no idea why his son had returned. For all he knew, the son had run out of money and come back to ask for more, as well as some clean clothes and a warm meal. He had no hint his son was returning to seek forgiveness and make things right with his dad. I wonder if, in his excitement, the father even heard his son say, "I've sinned."

As their reunion unfolded, the dad gave orders to his servants to bring special gifts to his son. The first gift, a robe, replaced the son's threadbare clothes. The original language describes this robe as a neck-to-ankle stole, an expensive garment reserved only for the most special occasions and the most special people. This gift symbolized the joy of forgiveness. Then his father gave him a signet ring of great value. Instead of a lecture, the son received a reminder of his father's love. Next the father placed sandals on his son's bare feet. This carried unique significance because only slaves went barefoot. The shoes spoke of the father's heart to receive his son not as a slave, but as his beloved son. As a final grace gift, the father ordered his servants to prepare a grand feast in his son's honor. It featured beef from a calf reserved only for use at special occasions.

The son deserved none of these gifts. He had brought his father shame and heartache and had wasted his inheritance. The point of Jesus's story, however, lies not in what the son did or didn't deserve. Rather, it depicts a father's kind, grace filled heart, the kind of heart only God can create in us when our daughters rebel.

Dads, when you extend this kind of unmerited love to your daughter, many benefits will flow into your relationship with her.

How to Apply Relational Life Preserver 5

In retrospect, I realize how these grace gifts kept Heather's and my difficult relationship alive when nothing else could. Your seemingly small gifts from the heart to your daughter can help your relationship in these ways.

1. **They put a face on Christ's unconditional love for your daughter.**

During a visit to Heather in one of her treatment program stays, I wrote the following in my journal.

Heather unloaded all kinds of garbage on us today. It really hurt. I had stood up for her so much. . . . For Heather it seems like love has to be earned and deserved. "Lord give us wisdom in helping her realize she doesn't have to earn it or deserve it."

For reasons we still don't fully understand, Heather felt that she had to earn love. Those feelings fueled her rebellion. When I gave her gifts unrelated to her behavior, in a small way I modeled how Jesus loved her unconditionally.

Jesus minced no words in Luke 6 when he explained that when we show kindness to anyone who treats us well, it's no big deal to God. But when we extend Christ's love to those who least deserve it, we become most like Him.

Guard against a subtle expectation or demand that your daughter return kindness to you for a kindness you extend to her. She may sense from you a Now-what-are-you-going-to-give-me? attitude. We must leave those expectations in God's hands.

When we give unconditionally, God can use those grace gifts to soften our daughters' hearts. Such gifts depict Jesus's teaching on giving a "cup of cold water" in His name. Whenever we do good for our daughters, we do so not to reward or encourage their ongoing rebellion, but to show them God's love.

2. They can reinforce good behavior.

On the flip side, we can give grace gifts or privileges *after* our daughters show a good attitude or act properly. This can motivate them to behave that way more often. It's important, however, not to convey an "if-then" attitude: *If you will treat me nicely, then I will treat you nicely.* Phil Waldrep counsels,

Some of us have used gifts as attempts to manipulate wayward family members. We have given in order to get something, or we have withheld gifts to make a point to or to punish them . . . .

96

[T]hink about what the person values and give a present that says, "I understand what's important to you, and I love you." Consider giving a present at a time that doesn't require one.[1]

Gifts given to express thanks after good behavior will reinforce future good behavior. Let's say it's 10:30 p.m. on a school night, and your daughter has talked on the phone for 5.67 hours. You tap on her door and say, "Honey, it's time to get off the phone."

She responds, "Sure, Dad. I know tomorrow's a school day, and I want to be rested for my classes. And, as you've told me before, teenagers generally need at least eight hours of sleep each night. I'm more than happy to get off the phone right now. Thank you so much for your kind reminder."

After you pick yourself up off the floor and slap yourself to make sure you're not dreaming, you realize that sometimes your daughter will not fight your every request. Dad, I know this scenario is a *huge* stretch, but I hope you get the point.

When something positive happens, reinforce her behavior with, "Honey, it means a lot to me when you respond with a kind attitude. Go ahead and talk another fifteen minutes. I love you."

I realize that when we extend grace like this, we may fear she'll abuse our goodwill. Sometimes she may. Don't let that stop you. Remember, these small gestures will bring more good into your relationship than harm.

3. They can motivate her to give grace gifts to you.

As I wrote this chapter, I looked at several colored Post-it notes Heather gave me over the years. I've mentioned these; I've taped them on my shelves next to my desk. The notes read, "I love you, Dad; Thanks, Dad; Thanks for being an example." Each of these tiny gifts brought hope to our relationship at that moment and helped her become less self-centered. She's given me dozens of these, many during our most trying days. Had I withheld my love from her then, I doubt I'd have these beautiful reminders of her love.

One of my favorite gifts, lost somewhere in our last move, was a pink, heart-shaped stone she found during her stay in Utah. She sent it to me in one of her letters, and I immediately taped it to my Daytimer notebook. For five years, every time I opened that book, God reminded me of His love for me and my love for her.

Grace gifts are like warm sunshine in a relationship. One author writes,

> We all need and want approval, acceptance, and validation from others. We will automatically gravitate toward sources that provide these needs. Like heliotropic plants that turn their flower heads toward and follow the sun throughout the day, people fixate on sources of emotional warmth and nourishment and follow those sources wherever they go. We also automatically return warmth for warmth. And the converse is true—coldness begets coldness. When those who are close to us do not react warmly toward us, we feel released to turn toward other sources of warmth to fix on and follow.[2]

4. They can encourage your daughter to change.

In the twelfth chapter of his letter to the Romans, the apostle Paul referred to a proverb written by King Solomon: "If your enemies are hungry, feed them. If they are thirsty, give them something to drink, and they will be ashamed of what they have done to you" (Romans 12:20 NLT).

Paul highlighted the scriptural principle that when we do wrong, our greatest need is repentance. Undeserved gifts for those who wrong us—in our case, our daughters—become tools in God's hands to help them see their sin and selfishness. When this happens, their repentance and the restoration of the relationship can follow.

Guard yourself, however, from unrealistic expectations. Paul Waldrep also writes,

> If we harbor hopes that our prodigals will change magically and make us happy, we will probably be very disappointed. Genuine love always involves risk: the risk that we won't be appreciated, the risk that we will receive anger in return for kindness, or the risk that as we move toward our prodigals, they will move farther apart.[3]

Don't give your daughter one gift and then decide to withhold future ones if she shows no change. It will take repeated gifts to soften her heart. It took numerous gifts (and much more) over six years to see lasting results in Heather.

5. They can picture what her life can become.

Robert L. Veninga captures how a gift can sometimes symbolize something hopeful.

> Sometimes a family member will present a symbolic gift and in so doing protect the family from a sense of hopelessness. If you were to walk through the corridors of a children's hospital on Christmas Eve, you would find rooms filled with symbolic gifts. You might see a bicycle given to a child who will walk again only if he is willing to undergo hours of painful therapy. Or you might find a sled given to a child who has barely enough strength to make it to the bathroom. Or you might see a severely diabetic youngster learning to master Monopoly even though her eyesight is beginning to fail.
>
> The cynic might ask what the utility of such gifts is, particularly if the boy can no longer walk or the girl can no longer see.
>
> But each gift is in hope. Its symbolic value far outweighs its utility. For when the child receives the bike, he can envision himself hustling over to a friend's house. When the sled is propped up in the

hospital room, it is a symbol that life will not always be spent with needles and diagnostic tests. When a Monopoly game is mastered by sight, there is a recognition that it can be played when the eyes fail.

When a family member presents a symbolic gift or quietly expresses optimism, it has a powerful effect on the entire family. Sometimes all it takes is the image of that loved one to engender a sense of confidence in the future.[4]

Toward the end of our difficulties with Heather, I bought her a small blue Kia car that captured my love for her. I purchased it from a private seller, a man about my age. As I finalized the offer, we learned that he bought the car for his daughter. Their relationship had soured, and he took it away from her. I felt his pain as he signed over the title. The contrast between our two situations reinforced in my mind the rightness of my decision. The gift symbolized a new, hopeful phase of Heather's life.

As you consider how to use gifts to connect with your daughter's heart, realize that the size or cost of the gift is not most important. We're not trying to buy love, only communicate it, and often the smallest gestures can leave the greatest impressions.

God portrayed the gift of unmerited love when he told the prophet Hosea to extend grace toward his adulterous wife. Through Hosea's example, God showed his love for his wayward people. Six simple words convey the depth of his love, "My love will know no bounds" (Hosea 14:4 NLT)

Mom's Tip

If you are your daughter's birth mom, consider a gift tied to her birth. Gifts such as bronzed baby shoes, a framed picture of her in your arms at birth, or an early preschool picture you frame could help renew the deep mother-daughter bond.

May our daughters experience that kind of "no bounds" love from us.

A word of caution about grace gifts: sometimes such gifts do not help the relationship. If they anger your daughter and result in greater defiance, reconsider them. Or, if your daughter misinterprets them as a form of unconditional love that enables her to continue her rebellion, rethink the wisdom of these gifts.

RELATIONSHIP LIFTERS

- What does your daughter like (such as jewelry, books, CDs)? Purchase something inexpensive that she enjoys and give it to her this week, no strings attached. If she asks why you did it, tell her, "Because I love you."
- Next week do the same thing . . . and the next . . . and the next . . . and the next.
- To mark a significant moment in her life, buy her a special ring and include with it a letter that describes your love for her.
- If you travel, bring her a gift each time you return home (and don't forget your other kids).
- Find a gift she gave you, even something insignificant. Put it where you can see it often to remind you about the principle in this chapter.

For Daughters

Once again, my life returned to the way it was. It seemed to be one big trap, a great string of events that followed no rhyme or reason. Often my life was like getting caught in a riptide: I struggled without footing to keep my head above water. I felt I had no control. Things just happened.

As I stared at the blindingly white walls in Boston, I wasn't surprised that I'd ended up there. I remember my room seemed like a large white coffin. The small window on the north wall was barred and locked shut. As the leaves of the dying tree outside rattled against the window, the cold, gloomy winter perfectly reflected what was happening to me inside. The room was bare, sparse. Its furnishings included a single bed and a nightstand, which were bolted to the pale gray linoleum floor. The stark white bathroom had the same stale, cold feeling of the room. The unbreakable mirror bolted to the wall prevented its use in a suicide attempt.

When I looked down the hall, I saw only an antiseptic whiteness made a glowing gray by the buzzing fluorescent lights. Sadness and anger lived in this place. Desperation was king.

I remember hearing a steady *thud! thud!* I got up from my bed and crept down the hall, carefully following the noise. It came from one of the rooms. I gently knocked and opened the door. Blood smears stained the wall. Her knuckles bled. She had punched the wall so hard that her blood and bits of skin remained plastered to those stark white walls. Red smeared on white.

Perhaps her bloody knuckles were her way of reminding herself that she was alive. Perhaps it wasn't about anger, or rebellion, or acting out. Maybe it was about seeing the lifeblood leave her body—at least she knew there was something in her that was still living.

I went back to my room.

I'd been admitted to the hospital in Boston for "psychiatric evaluation," meaning my parents wanted an explanation for the reason I was so bent on defying their wishes. I had been at the hospital for one night, and I expected a visit from my dad soon. I will never forget that visit.

I'd become so accustomed to strange noises that when he knocked, I didn't respond, so he opened the door. I looked up, and there stood my dad. His red-rimmed blue eyes looked distant, and at the same time, fearful. He managed a weak smile.

"Hi, Dad," I mumbled.

"Hi, Heather."

We didn't say much to each other. We were at odds, to say the least. We both felt angry, hurt, and confused. Our relationship had all but ceased to be. Our eyes met. I looked away.

"I brought something for you," he said.

It caught me off guard. I didn't expect anything, and I surely didn't deserve anything.

He stepped out of the room and returned with a huge card. In black and white, the card showed a smiling Chihuahua standing in a pair of oversized Converses. On the front it read, "Hurry and get well" . . . I opened it, and it continued, "Nobody else could fill your shoes!" He signed it, "Love, Dad."

In hindsight, I realize that simply signing the card *love, Dad* was a huge step and a great sacrifice for my father. He and I were in the midst of one of the most difficult times in our relationship, and he willingly extended himself to me. The tiny note *Love, Dad* spoke volumes.

As I blankly stared at the card, through all the anger and bitterness against my father a bit of feeling began to peek its way into my heart like a light at the end of a tunnel. My voice caught in my throat.

"Thanks, Dad."

I had just cost him thousands of dollars to send me to that place. He'd just spent hundreds to fly to Boston, to get a hotel room, and to rent a car. He'd taken off work. And, though I'd already cost so much time, money, and especially emotional effort, he was still reaching out to me. This simple gift spoke of hope. Perhaps, somehow and in some way, our relationship would survive. This card (which I still keep in my room) showed me that love and life still lingered in our relationship. It wasn't over yet.

The little ray of sunshine that accompanied that card seemed garishly out of place. That wasn't a happy place. I set the card against the wall and kept it there. My roommate, a victim of sexual and physical abuse of the worst kind, talked about it. She loved it. It brought life to our stark white room. Although it seemed like putting a Band-Aid on a gaping stab wound, it still brought healing to my relationship with my dad.

Several times during my crazy years, my dad's little gifts breathed life into our suffocating relationship. Once, my family and I took a trip to Callaway Gardens, a well-known flower park in Georgia. At that time I was obsessed with butterflies. The garden's special attraction was its butterfly terrarium, a huge greenhouse visitors walk through. There, hundreds of butterflies circled overhead and landed on the exotic flowers.

I enjoyed the terrarium. But, as usual, once the family had finished what I wanted to do, I became a brat—pouting, stomping around, and sighing dramatically. After we walked around the garden for a while, we arrived at the gift shop. My eyes lit up when I saw a beautiful butterfly mobile. It was expensive, though, and I didn't have a steady income at the age of fourteen. So what was my idea of "compromise"? I demanded that my parents buy it for me. They immediately said no because my actions that day hadn't earned any gifts. I sulked, rolled my eyes, made a scene, gave my last glare (and tried all the other tricks I used to get my way) to no avail. I then stomped back to the car to seethe.

My family returned about twenty minutes later. When my dad opened the car door closest to me, I expected him to give me "the talk" about my attitude. Instead, he handed me a daintily wrapped box topped with a shiny bow. I opened the gift. It was the butterfly mobile. He said, "I just wanted to get this for you." I sat there with the box in my hands, speechless. I was shocked. I didn't deserve the mobile. But he bought it for me in spite of my actions simply because he loved me.

Throughout my rebellious years, these small gifts communicated my dad's love for me. I didn't earn his love, and I surely didn't deserve it. But through his gifts he gave it anyway.

Gifts often communicate what words can't on their own. The Bible gives us a beautiful example of this in a Hallmark moment story about a woman who gave a special gift to Jesus.

Jesus was invited to dinner at a Pharisee's house. The Pharisees in Jesus's day were a pompous, self-righteous group of religious zealots. A prostitute who had experienced Jesus's forgiveness heard about his visit there. Much to the dismay of the Pharisees, she entered the house where they were eating. She brought with her an alabaster jar full of expensive perfume that cost an entire year's income. This special perfume was designed for special occasions due to its high cost; however, without a word, the prostitute approached Jesus, broke open the alabaster jar, and poured the oil on his feet. As she did this, she began weeping. As her tears fell on Jesus's feet, she began to kiss them and wipe them with her hair. She subjected herself to the whispers and stares of the Pharisees and the chance that Jesus would shun her, a prostitute. But out of love she gave Him the most valuable possession she owned: her alabaster jar of perfume.

Although she gave her most valuable possession, the story doesn't imply that you must give your dad the same. Rather, it describes how love can motivate us to give tangible expressions of our love. Even though you may not feel love toward your dad, he needs to know that you do love him. Gifts can tell him this when maybe you can't say it. You'd be surprised how much your gifts will mean to him.

I remember a "gift" I gave my dad that I didn't think too much about but that meant the world to him. When I was in Utah, they made us rake a huge gravel parking lot (once again, avoid wilderness camps!). The gravel was composed of many different colored rocks. One day as I raked, I looked down and spied a pink rock. I picked it up and dusted it off, and noticed that it looked like a heart. I stuck it in my back pocket.

That evening, as I wrote my daily letter home, I dug the rock out of my jeans and placed it in the envelope. I wrote, *Dad, this heart rock is for you. I love you.* Though it was only a silly rock, he kept it rock taped to his daily calendar for years. He treasured that tiny rock because it reminded him that I still loved him.

See, dads are easy—even the smallest extension of yourself, the smallest gift, the smallest gesture can make their day. They don't need expensive or fancy things, just simple gifts from your heart that assure them that you do love them, even though you may not always act like it.

Though they're small, these gifts can do wonders to mend your relationship. When I remember the gifts that meant the most to me, they meant so much not because they were flashy or expensive, but because someone gave them from his or her heart. Those small gifts my dad gave me, such as the butterfly mobile, the card, and a certain stuffed caterpillar, meant more to me than their intrinsic value. They were signs of hope and of love.

Gifts from you to your dad can give him those same feelings. A homemade card can become a little memento of better times. My dad's favorites? Small neon Post-it notes with little notes scrawled on them. He keeps every one. You don't have to spend exorbitant amounts of money. When you want to give your dad something that shows you love him, listen to your heart.

A few cautions, though.

First of all, don't give your dad something to manipulate him. Don't say, "Oh, here, Dad! Look what I got you! Can I use the car/ have some money/get a tattoo?" Give because you want to give, not because you want something in return.

Secondly, don't use your gifts against him. When he says, "Honey, extending your curfew by four hours is a little excessive," don't say, "Well! I made you a card! I'm never doing that again!" These gifts are not bribery or "brownie points"—they're to show selfless love toward your dad.

Finally, don't withhold gifts until he gives you something first. When he gives you gas money, don't say, "Oh, here, Dad! Look what I got for you!" How would you feel if your dad did something nice for you only when you did something nice for him? This isn't the way it works. Give because you love him.

Relationship Lifters

- Does your dad like to fish? Does he enjoy football games? Computers? Get him a little something that relates to his hobby, perhaps a key chain or a card. It's not about how much it costs; it's about the heart behind it.
- Make your dad a card. I made my dad several I decorated with glitter, stickers, and so on. Even though they were some of the ugliest cards he'd ever seen, he loved them anyway. It doesn't matter if you can't draw. He'll still love it.
- Offer to take your dad out. Go on a walk, go get ice cream, go see a movie—and pay for it yourself! You don't have to talk that much. Your willingness and desire to spend time with him will speak more to him than your words.

Mom to Mom

Mom, you constantly give. It seems like a 24/7 job. If things go as expected, we assume we'll enjoy the dividends of our labor. If your daughter rebels and things don't go as planned, those hoped-for dividends seem like they will never materialize. When that happens the last thing you feel like doing is continuing to give. Although we may want to retreat into our emotional bunkers to avoid another round of attack, Christ shows us another way through His example.

John 13 describes Jesus's last supper with His disciples. He already knew what the next twelve hours would bring, including Judas's heart-wrenching betrayal. Even so, He humbled Himself before all the disciples and washed their feet. When everything told Jesus to stop loving, He continued to love and give anyway.

Verse 1 gives the key to understanding this unexpected act. It says that Jesus knew where He had come from and where He was going. This perspective gave Him this great love in troubled times.

Similarly, we can show Christ's love when our daughters act like Judas. It begins with prayer that God will open our daughters' hearts with Christ's love. Unexpected gifts can help bring this about: finding her laundry neatly folded on her bed, a vase of fresh flowers in her bathroom, a note under her pillow. Such simple tokens can remind her of your love and soften her heart.

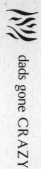
A Mother's Prayer

Dear Father,
I am grateful for the many ways
You have shown me Your love
when I've rebelled against You.
Help me reflect that same love
to my rebellious one.

six

I SCREWED SHUT HER WINDOWS AND SHE STILL ESCAPED

Laughter is the shortest distance between two people.
—Victor Borge[1]

Against the assault of laughter, nothing can stand.
—Mark Twain, *The Mysterious Stranger*

For Dads

The phone jarred us awake at 5 a.m. that Easter Sunday. Groggily my wife answered it, and after a slight pause she said, "Of course Heather's at home." As she slammed the receiver down in frustration, she mumbled, "I can't believe it. A neighbor just called and asked if Heather was in bed." We numbly rolled over to go back to sleep, shaking off what seemed like an intrusive question.

After a few moments we simultaneously bolted upright. I flipped on the nightstand light. We looked at each other with dread in our eyes. "Oh no!" we both said. I threw back the covers and tossed off my sleep mask. With my Breathe Right nasal strip still in place, I snorted, "She'd better be there." I somersaulted over Sherryl (okay, maybe I just crawled over her), and she trailed me as we dashed to Heather's room.

When I found her door locked, I tapped lightly and in a syrupy voice asked, "Heather, sweetie, are you there?" Silence followed.

With a slightly raised voice I again asked, "Heather, are you there?" No answer. As our fears began to mount, my blood pressure spiraled upward and I fumbled to find the L-shaped safety key above the doorframe. I finally inserted it into the door handle, unlocked the door, and flicked on the light.

As a pastor, I had looked forward to that particular Easter with great anticipation. We were going to celebrate Jesus's resurrection in our brand-new church building. Of course, Easter Sunday always brought big crowds, and preachers *love* big crowds. I needed to be at my best for that day.

We couldn't have timed opening her door more perfectly. As the room light came on, there sat our Easter surprise: Heather was straddling the second-floor sill—one combat-boot-wearing foot planted on the floor and the other dangling outside. She was as shocked as we were.

"Well, take a look at that. The Easter bunny has arrived," said Sherryl. I couldn't help but snicker. We had caught Heather red-handed sneaking in after a night out doing who knows what, who knows where.

Fortunately, my wife's humor eased the tension enough for me to stay calm. I needed to, because in a few hours I would stand before hundreds of worshipers who expected a "happy" Easter message from a "happy" pastor. But later that afternoon, after I took a short fitful nap, my anger finally surfaced. *How dare my daughter sneak out at night the night before Easter Sunday—our biggest day of the year?* She had gotten out before; this was the last straw. Up to that point I didn't know how she did it. We had equipped our home with an alarm system we armed each night. However, we hadn't installed sensors on the second floor windows. So Heather was able to sneak out without activating the alarm.

(I wished I had had another family's foresight. To prepare for the possibility that their preschoolers might want to sneak out when they became teenagers, the parents planted cactus plants below each window. However, I don't advocate that technique today).

As I stewed, an idea came to my mind—one I was convinced would guarantee that Heather never snuck out again.

A trip to Home Depot that afternoon to buy key materials to execute my plan boosted my confidence. I purchased a box of four-inch, galvanized screws and a Phillips drill bit. I collected my ten-foot aluminum ladder, my Craftsman drill, the box of screws, and an extension cord. With each step of my plan, I grew more certain I could corral this daughter and force her into "Christian" submission.

I crept outside and leaned the ladder against the front of the house, plugged in my extension cord and drill, and began my cage-the-wild-animal project. I drilled two pilot holes in each window sill and then tightly screwed in the four-inch screws to permanently close her windows.

(I realize that this is a serious safety issue, should there have been a house fire or some other reason to escape quickly. I don't recommend it! But I was thinking of only one goal at that time.)

Ah ha! I thought to myself. *My superior intelligence and brilliant plan has solved our escapee problem for good.* With smug confidence I believed Heather would never escape again. How wrong I was.

A few days afterward I tried to open the window in my office on the basement level of our home. It stuck shut. With enough elbow grease, however, I finally opened it. As I did, a bead of caulk sheared off the bottom of the window sill. I thought that was odd but figured it must have somehow bled out of the window frame. I faced the same recurring problem for the next two years. I didn't realize until years later that Heather had outwitted me.

When she and I began to write this book, she revealed that even after I had screwed her windows shut, she still sneaked out at will. How? Through quite an ingenious plan, actually. By caulking the bottom part of my office window shut, she could slide down the top half of the window without opening the bottom half that would trigger the alarm. When she told me this, I burst out laughing. Sometimes I guess it's good not to know every crazy thing your daughter does.

During our difficult years, because I was constantly overwhelmed by the serious nature of the rebellion, God brought moments of humor into our relationship to ease the tension. Some dads tend to wallow in the relational pain their daughters cause. When that happens, too often we can create a gloomy, negative atmosphere that lingers 24/7. However, when by God's grace we find humor in those difficult moments, it provides a counterbalance to the negative emotions that can cripple us.

Mom's Tip

Mom, either you or your husband has a greater sense of humor. Whoever does will need to actively bring the humor into your difficulties with your daughter. Talk about this with your husband, and the two of you determine who that is.

The Bible often speaks of joy and laughter as a counter-balance to difficulty and pain. The word "laugh" appears first in Genesis 17:17, when God informed one-hundred-year-old Abraham his ninety-year-old wife would give birth to a son. God even commanded Abraham to name his son *Isaac*, which in Hebrew means "God's laugh." Humor writer Cal Samra notes, "It is no small matter that in its very first book, the Bible establishes, very quickly, the image of a loving God who has a sense of humor and who laughs."[2]

Over fifty references to laughter appear in the Old Testament. The books of Psalms, Proverbs, and Song of Solomon have descriptions of the laughter of God. Ecclesiastes 3:4 declares that there is a "time to laugh." David, Jeremiah, and Daniel all wrote about laughter. The New Testament records more than 250 references to joy, gladness, rejoicing, and laughter. Celebration filled the air at the births of John the Baptist and Jesus. Jesus performed his first miracle at a time of great happiness—a wedding. The Beatitudes in Jesus's famous Sermon on the Mount all begin with "blessed," which some Bible versions translate as "happy."

Shortly before Jesus's crucifixion, He explained to His disciples that He would soon die. As sadness and fear settled into their hearts, Jesus reminded them to stand strong in Him and continue to obey His commands. He then interjected a prediction all the more profound because He knew the crucifixion awaited Him. He said, "I have told you this so that you will be filled with my joy. Yes, your joy will overflow!" (John 15:11 NLT). Even though Jesus faced mockery, scourging, denial, betrayal, rejection, false accusations, and crucifixion, He spoke of joy. But He didn't keep it to Himself. He told His disciples (and us) to find our joy in His, just as tree branches draw their life from the trunk of the tree.

The humorless Pharisees criticized Jesus because He associated with sinners. But those sinners loved to hang around Him because He exuded joy. Dr. Humphrey Osmond writes, "Jesus had an excellent sense of humor and pungent wit. If He hadn't, He could not have made such a favorable impression on publicans and sinners, and such an unfavorable impression on the religious establishment. The gospel brought glad tidings."[3]

Jesus knew best how to use humor to maximize its impact. Remember the scene in *The Passion of the Christ* where we got a glimpse of Jesus's playfulness when He splashed water on Mary's face? Jesus was playful. He attracted children because children are attracted to those who love to laugh. No one would have wanted to be with someone who wasn't joy-filled.

Laughter, even in the difficult times with your daughter, will help you maintain your relationship with her. One study of adolescent attitudes toward their fathers listed "a sense of humor" as one of the top ten things fathers did right.[4] Consider these simple pointers to help you laugh between the tears.

How to Apply Relational Life Preserver 6

1. Be fun to live with.

Nobody likes to be around uptight, negative, overly serious people. I remember my father as a very positive person. He loved to laugh and act goofy. One time he and a friend dressed as the world's ugliest women for a church Valentine costume party. Everybody about died laughing because they played their roles so well.

I cherish that about my dad, and he hasn't lost a bit of that spirit. His love for laughter rubbed off on our family; we laugh a lot in our home. I admit, though, that laughter came less frequently during Heather's difficult years. When we did interject humor, it took the edge off our relational tension.

Ask yourself if you're fun to live with. Better yet, ask your daughter. If you find your home always filled with tension and heaviness, be silly with your girl. Laugh with her, and fill your home with joy.

2. Practice laughing.

How do you respond when your daughter pushes your buttons? Do you get angry and blow up? Do you become sullen and withdraw from her? Do you take out your frustration on other members of your family? We must become aware of our normal responses first before we can change them.

The next time she frustrates you, look for something in that situation that can bring a smile or a chuckle. One woman asked a friend when she had learned to laugh. She responded, "I began to laugh when my life was in a state of total disaster."[5]

Develop a sense of humor. Read a Dave Barry book. Listen to Garrison Keillor's *A Prairie Home Companion* on public radio. Read the comics each day to get a chuckle. Try to laugh at least three times daily.

3. Don't limit your identity to that of being just "a parent."

S. Rutherford McDill, a counselor, writes,

Mom's Tip

Mom, the above temptation may nag you more than it nags your husband, especially if you're a stay-at-home mom. Develop interests outside your role as a parent. Take up a hobby, join a health club, or volunteer at

Consciously remind yourself of the other aspects of your life. Your parenting self is just a small part of your total self. . . . The dangerous parent is the one whose life has shrunk to the point where he or she is a parent only. . . . When you develop your total self you enlarge your identity. You live in dimensions of life that are entirely outside of your prodigal's crises. From those dimensions you find strength to wag your head and wonder how your prodigal does it, how he finds the seemingly limit-

less ways to get himself into one pickle after another. You might even find yourself chuckling.[6]

4. Laugh at yourself.

We once received a call from the police that Heather was involved in a car wreck that resulted in a fight with an adult. I quickly drove to the accident site and found Heather in the back of a police cruiser with an ambulance parked nearby. As the police cruiser lights illuminated my embarrassed face, gawkers stood around to observe. A wrecker was taking away a car with its front end smashed and a pile of bricks littered a once-attractive mailbox area. The officer explained that Heather would not be charged because she was just a passenger. She would, however, have to deal with the adult with whom she scuffled.

Then, a woman walked toward me from the crowd. She asked, "What happened, Pastor Stone?" I gulped when I saw who she was—my former church secretary. I think God enjoyed a chuckle from that incident.

When the fur flies, it's easy to slip into end-of-the-world thinking. When that happens, don't take things so seriously. Samra wisely points out that "humor can be a healthy strategy for letting off steam, and while it may be demeaning to poke fun at others, we might all benefit by poking fun at ourselves on occasion."[7]

5. Laugh with your daughter.

One of the qualities of a healthy, functional family is sharing humor. Says Norm Wright: "Family members can laugh together, and they enjoy life together."[8] When our family laughs together, and not at each other, it bonds us together. It refreshes us like rain on parched ground.

Heather once worked at a nursing home and often told me funny accounts of what happened there. She described an incident when a resident had fallen and couldn't get up. Another resident with a walker hobbled over to allay her fears. She leaned down, put her feeble hand on her friend, and yelled, "Don't worry, Nellie! I've called 8-1-1!" We both got a kick out of that story. When I laugh with Heather, it always strengthens our relationship.

Dallas Willard says that "genuine shared laughter is one of the surest ways for human beings to come together and break the stalemates of life. It is essential to genuine community."[9]

6. Don't use laughter to demean or provoke your daughter.

Jesus never laughed at a hurting or ill person. His humor, rather, lifted up the downcast and often put the high and mighty Pharisees in their place.

Unfortunately, much of the so-called humor modeled for us today comes from TV sitcoms. Most of that is insult humor that makes fun of someone else. In real life, many of us would feel deeply hurt with such cutting remarks.

Hurting people hurt others with their humorous sarcasm, barbs, and putdowns. We must never use humor that way. Rather, we must laugh with our daughters and never at them. Otherwise we'll pay dearly.

Humor and laughter, properly used, can soften those difficult moments with our daughters because it often can give us a lift in the midst of our worries. So remember, if an Easter bunny surprises you one day and shows up at your door (or on your window sill) looking like your daughter, don't over react. Allow humor to soften your anger as Sherryl did for us. You'll be glad you did.

Relationship Lifters

- This week, check the Sunday comic strips. Cut out the ones that make you laugh and tape them to your daughter's bedroom door or bathroom mirror.
- Ask her to describe the most humorous thing you ever did in response to one of her rebellious moments. Don't defend yourself, but try to find humor in it as well.
- See if she'd be open to the two of you going on a "date" to see a funny movie together.
- Get a *Far Side* calendar for the both of you. Talk about the ones that bring a smile.

For Daughters

I tiptoed around my room so that my parents wouldn't wake up. I had already reapplied my thick black eyeliner and laced up my Docs. As I tugged on my fuzzy leopard-print micromini in the dark, I heard a pebble hit my window, then another.

That was the signal. I slid open my window. Underneath the window stood Derik, my pink-mohawked, pierced, tattooed boyfriend of less than a month. (They hardly ever made it past thirty days.)

I leaned my head out the window and whispered, "Coming!"

I was the teenage MacGyver. Outfitted in my barely there outfit, I deftly swung myself out of my second-story window and onto the roof. I scrambled up one side and down the other. Then came the ten-foot drop from the roof to the fence. Derik waited for me below the roof. I grabbed onto the shingles and the gutter (I always wondered if my parents noticed that the gutter was bent into a *V* only in that spot) and slid my body down, scraping myself across the shingles, until I could almost feel the fence beneath my feet. I crouched on the fence and jumped the ten feet down. I kissed Derik hello, and we took off down the driveway.

Then *it* happened. A light flashed on and quickly illuminated the upstairs window. *Oh, no. Not this!* The garage door rumbled open. I didn't run because I knew I had been caught. My dad had actually taken down my friends' license plate numbers at one time so he could track down the car I'd hop in. I knew that trying to escape was futile.

You know that Christmas poem "The Night Before Christmas" about Santa Claus?

When out on the lawn there arose such a clatter,
I sprang from my bed to see what was the matter.

120

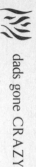

Away to the window I flew like a flash,
Tore open the shutters and threw up the sash ...

Well, the narrator in that poem must have been one of my dad's ancestors. Outfitted in his *Good Night Charles* T-shirt and matching star-speckled *Good Night Charles* boxers (I am not making this up), he dashed up the driveway, his skinny bird legs (which I inherited) propelling him as fast as they could go. The flaps from his sleep mask whipped behind him like the streamers on the handles of a kid's bike. His eyes were as big as saucers, and the Breathe Right strip plastered to his nose only made his already-enormous-from-anger-and-panting nostrils even larger. In his left hand he carried his heavy-duty, blind-any-boys-that-come-to-pick-up-my-daughter-at-midnight flashlight and in the other some papers and a pen.

I can only imagine that he felt like Zorro on a mission to save his daughter from the bad guys. He immediately began his line of questioning: "I am Heather's father! Who are you? Where did you come from? Are you on drugs? Who are your parents? Where do you live? Do you attend church? What is your GPA? What is your Social Security number? Was it your intention to dye your hair neon pink? Does your nose ring serve a meaningful purpose?" I mean, as if my boyfriend at the time would have answered truthfully.

I'd just been caught sneaking out, although my dad hadn't yet figured out for sure that the window was my primary escape route. He would later catch me red-handed, though.

Because my parents had grown weary of the late-night Heather roundups, my dad began to plan ahead. He installed locks on the inside of my windows to make sure I wouldn't sneak out that way.

Right . . . like locks were going to stop me. My sidekick Misty and I used a screwdriver to crack them and pop them off. When he finally caught me as I used the window to return from an escape one Easter morning, Dad realized his plan had failed. So that time, he used screws.

He actually screwed my windows shut from the outside. Since there was no way to undo this, Misty and I collaborated and hatched our plan. We would escape through a window downstairs. Since our house had an alarm system, we had to work around the alarm or we'd get busted. After some careful experimentation, we discovered that the windows downstairs could be opened from the top without triggering the alarm. After rummaging around in the basement for a while for some ideas, we found our tool—caulk. I still don't exactly know what it's used for, but I decided it would work well for our purposes. We opened the bottom half of the downstairs window (the one in my dad's office, of all places) and gooped as much caulk as we could on the window sill. And ta-da! After we let it dry for the recommended twenty-four hours, we could successfully sneak out of the top window to meet our hoodlum boyfriends without setting off the alarm!

Now, don't get any ideas. Although I'm retelling this as a funny story, at the time I was mad. When my plans to sneak out at night were thwarted, I usually went ballistic on Dad. In the moment, I didn't find any humor in the situation. I probably screamed, cursed, and resigned myself to pouting in my room as I organized my next plan. However, had I been sorry for what I'd done and noticed how funny my dad looked as he ran up the driveway, I probably would have laughed and perhaps come out of the situation in a better frame of mind.

You may encounter some unpleasant situations in your relationship with your dad, such as being out after curfew, getting grounded, arguing over boys. When you do, if you can allow yourself to laugh instead of taking things so seriously, it will help you keep perspective.

The Bible talks a lot about laughter. The word "laugh" is even mentioned in the very first book of the Bible (Genesis 17:17). In Ecclesiastes 3:4, the Bible even says there is a "time to laugh."

I personally can't believe that Jesus didn't have a sense of humor. Have you ever seen a kiwi bird? A praying mantis? Or a hairless cat? Have you ever heard a guinea hen? Or a guinea pig? As a kid, I had three guinea pigs. Their noise productions ranged from Nintendo-like squeaks and chirps to the shrill *reek! reek! reek!* of a siren when they got frightened. They're hilarious! To create and design each and every one of these creatures, God must have had a sense of humor.

Many times, we make God out to be this humongous, frightening, impersonal bearded old guy with a booming Charlton Heston voice and a giant scepter with which to knock us over the head. God became a simple human being—and He was joyful, happy, and playful. Even children were drawn to Him and adored Him.

So when you're in the midst of some crazy, knockdown fight with your dad, calm down, and lighten up. Remember—it's not the end of the world. Maybe you can use these few tips to add humor to the difficult times in your relationship.

Don't take things so seriously—relax!

I once lived a few houses down from someone we called "the cat lady." She was very compassionate, a PETA role model who found and adopted a new stray cat each week. But there was one cat, the worst, named Gabrielle.

Gabrielle was *evil.* This cat could easily have been the star of the *Pet Cemetery* movie or a story entitled "When Bad Cats Happen to Innocent Neighbors." "Gaby" walked around with a smug, I-dare-you look on its face. It hissed when you came near it, then demanded that you pet it. If your fingers hung around for too long, however, this cat would make sure they weren't obstructing her sunlight. It walked all over our cars, taunted our dogs, and deliberately laid in front of our tires—as we were starting to move. (Yes, I was tempted). Needless to say, we all were desperate for some rabid pit bull to tear the thing to bits.

After a disappointing hit-and-miss with Gabrielle, it dawned on me—I had acted just like that cat! I would be happy and smiling, but as soon as Dad came around and told me something I didn't want to hear, I'd turn into the "cat from hell": snobby, demanding, irritable, and just plain obnoxious. Why? I just wanted to make my dad miserable. That was absolutely pointless. Launching into "jerk mode" didn't benefit anybody, least of all me. I must have looked ridiculous pacing around the kitchen, tossing things around noisily, sighing loudly, and throwing a childish fit all because my dad asked me to empty the dishwasher. I should have seen how immature and silly I was acting; if I had I would have laughed at myself.

Watch out for the jerk transformation, and put a stop to it before it's complete. Don't let your attitude mimic that of the cat all our neighbors wanted to run over.

Learn to laugh with your dad (no matter how un-funny he is).

When I was in my "dark years" (I guess you could call them that), I took everything seriously. I was too preoccupied with sulking or plotting another diabolical escape route that I never lightened up enough to realize that my dad was actually kind of funny (in a weird way).

For instance, one thing he did embarrassed and angered me to no end—his now infamous "old man" impression. His favorite place to perform this act was the local mall. He hiked his pants up to his chest, hunched over, bowed his legs, and shuffled down the food court, while he chewed on his tongue and proudly proclaimed, "This is my daughter!" It horrified me. I eventually stormed off in a rage to punish my dad and make the family miserable for the rest of the night. I didn't realize that people were not looking at me. No. They were laughing at the bizarre crazy man, drooling and mumbling nonsense.

Well, my dad never grew out of the old-man-impersonation phase. But now when he does it, I just laugh at him. Instead of being worried about what people think of me, I laugh at all the confused and fearful stares of people looking at him. Who cares that my dad acts weird? My dad didn't think studded belts and piercings were cool, but he dealt with them anyway. *All* dads act weird; it's part of their fatherly duty to be embarrassing and corny. So just let him be himself—and laugh with him.

And last but not least, don't laugh *at* your dad when you're not supposed to.

If he's trying to talk to you about something that's important to him, don't laugh at him. Do your best to treat your dad the way you'd want him to treat you.

I mocked my dad by impersonating him (in a bad way), laughing at the things he said, making fun of his beliefs, rolling my eyes at the things he said, and so on. I was not lighthearted and humorous; I was just plain disrespectful.

If you want to improve your relationship with your dad, make sure you show him the respect he deserves. It's okay to joke around and have a good time, but make sure that you don't take it too far.

Relationship Lifters

- Watch a funny movie with your dad. Keep in mind that it should be dad-friendly. For instance, most dads would probably find *American Pie* offensive. Don't watch it with him. (Or ever. It's a terrible, tacky movie). Try something like *A Bug's Life* (one of my dad's favorites) or a Steve Martin movie.

- Accept your differences ... and laugh at them. For instance, your dad's idea of great music may be played on National Public Radio at 3 a.m., whereas yours may be someone on the bill at Coachella or the Warped Tour. It's okay! Learn to accept and laugh at each other's differences. Just be respectful. And who knows ... maybe old Barry Manilow will grow on you—maybe.
- Get your dad a funny card. My room is unusually trashed. I am convinced that I have received from my dad every card in existence regarding unclean rooms. It's a sort of inside joke that we share. Is your dad obsessed with the remote? Does he have any strange quirks (yes—all dads do)? Find a card relating to them and give it to him as a surprise.

Mom to Mom

As I journeyed through Heather's intense rebellion, I found very little to laugh about. The daily stress and heartbreak pulverized my emotions into chopped liver. I felt fragile and bruised, sustained only by God's grace and my friends' and family's prayers. God always met my every need and sometimes used laughter to do it. As Proverbs 17:22 tells us, "A cheerful heart is good medicine, but a crushed spirit dries up the bones."

Sometimes my laughter erupted at the most unexpected times. One morning after Heather's not-to-be-trusted girlfriend and her suspicious-looking boyfriend picked her up for school, I called a friend to tell her what had happened. As I described how I had run outside to question her before she left, I imagined the scene. I saw myself bolt from the house in my bright purple robe and mismatched fuzzy slippers, with disheveled hair and arms waving as I ran up the driveway. I imagined myself as an evil Barney out to terrorize the neighborhood. Sometimes the Lord will give you moments like these to lighten your heart's heavy load. Capture them when they come.

A Mother's Prayer

*Lord, thank You for laughter
in spite of my tears.
Bring laughter into my life today,
and help me embrace it as You fill
me with Your joy.*

seven

THE WAR ZONE

If you can cut it off, wash it out, or grow it out,
don't sweat it![1]

For Dads

[WARNING! What you're about to read may be shocking. Read the entire chapter before drawing conclusions.]

I couldn't believe what I was about to do. No turning back now. I planned to leave after dark to minimize the chance of being sighted. (I learned the under-the-cover-of-darkness technique from my then-favorite TV show, *The X-Files*. We pastors learn lots of good stuff from great theologians such as Mulder and Scully.)

At dusk my passenger and I jumped into my dark blue Mazda. I paused and asked myself one last time, *Charles, are you sure you want to do this? Is this stupid or what?*

No thunder or lightning bolts from God. I had to go with that. We backed out into the street. I looked left and right. *Good, an empty street. No one to see me. No silhouette peering out from beneath the streetlight.* I didn't speak to my passenger. The mission to the destination point took only five minutes.

I wheeled into the dimly lit parking lot. *Good, the dry cleaners and the karate studio next door are closed. The pizza shop is far enough away so no one there can see me.* I idled into an empty spot and noticed only one other car nearby. As I stepped out, the cold wind slapped me in the face, as if to ask, *What would a church member think, Mr. Pastor?*

I zipped up my brown parka and pulled up the collar around my face. With a final furtive look to my left and right, I pushed open the smudged glass door. The naked fluorescent lights and the musty smell made me feel creepy. My heart began to pound. My palms began to sweat, and my breathing became shallow. My parched throat made swallowing difficult.

Compose yourself, Charles. Don't back out now.

I walked over to the candy counter to avoid arousing the suspicion of the unshaven, greasy-haired clerk. After trying to look interested in a Snickers bar, I knew it was now or never. This deal was going down.

I made my move. I marched to the cluttered counter. I pointed and pulled out a five. "Bag, please," I muttered and snatched it out of his hands before somebody else came in. I crumpled the brown paper around my purchase and crammed it into my parka pocket. I scanned the store once more.

Good, no one's here. I didn't get caught. Mulder would be proud.

I scrambled out of the store, jumped into my old Mazda, and squealed out of the parking lot. I think I hit sixty in about twenty-four seconds. Once I cleared the intersection, my heart rate dropped below the attack zone. I reached into my jacket, pulled out the bag, and threw it to my companion. "There, Heather. I hope you enjoy your . . . cigarettes."

My mission that evening? To

Mom's Tip

Mom, the cigarette purchase may seem disturbing, but what battle, within reason, should you lose with your daughter to help you ultimately win the war?

purchase a pack of Newports for my sixteen-year-old daughter.

I'd not come that close to a cigarette since curiosity about smoking picqued my interest at age ten. One day I had picked up a still-smoldering cigarette from the street and held it about three inches from my mouth (I didn't want my lips to touch the lipstick-stained butt). With all my might, I huffed and puffed to inhale some smoke. I almost passed out from hyperventilation. After that, I didn't even want to touch what my dad called "cancer sticks."

I hated cigarettes then and still do now. They stink and rot your lungs. They turn your fingernails yellow and give you prune skin. But that night, with the one-and-only purchase of a pack of cigarettes for my daughter, I put into practice an invaluable lesson. To win the ultimate war with a difficult daughter, sometimes we must choose to lose a few battles—battles that may make us sacrifice beyond what we can imagine.

Do I advocate buying your kids cigarettes? Absolutely not. Would I ever do it again? I doubt it. I never bought Heather cigarettes again, and she doesn't smoke today. My wife and I agreed to buy the cigarettes because Heather was about to enter a rehab program. She told us that she'd do drugs if she didn't have cigarettes. I do, however, advocate that dads carefully choose their battles and lose some so they can ultimately win the war.

❖

As I look back at my parenting, I realize that Heather was our "experimental child." The firstborn child often gets the brunt of people's attempts to figure out parenting. My biggest mistake with Heather? My need to be in control. I now realize that I set up too many restrictions for Heather, hoping that I would protect her from danger and evil.

In her early years my list of prohibited toys and TV included the Care Bears (toys that had an element of magic, which I thought would lead Heather to experiment with drugs); My Little Pony (magical toy unicorns that the evil Care Bears probably rode on); Jem (a cartoon whose main character wore a miniskirt, probably because she dabbled in magic she learned from a unicorn-riding Care Bear); or *The Little Mermaid* (it had warlocks, which mean magic, and you know what magic does). I confess that I made too many issues a big deal. While I attended seminary a fellow student took his control issues to such an extreme that he literally threw his television out his window. I guess he didn't want his kids influenced by Care Bears or My Little Pony either.

Fortunately, I lightened up and learned to compromise during Heather's difficult years. I also began to understand several crucial parenting Scriptures that I failed to grasp in the earlier years.

Two key passages speak directly to fathers. Ephesians 6:4 says, "Fathers, do not exasperate your children; instead, bring them up in the training and instruction of the Lord." This statement was revolutionary because in biblical days fathers wielded absolute authority over their families. They literally held the power of life and death over them. The apostle Paul countered the culture with the view that a man didn't have to act like a tyrant.

When Heather was young, I placed too much emphasis on the last half of the verse: "training," which means discipline, and "instruction," which means to teach children right from wrong. I wanted her to make right choices and thought that my control would guarantee she'd go in the right direction. I used this tactic too far into her teen years. As a result I began to "exasperate" her, which incited her anger into full-fledged resentment toward me. The New

Mom's Tip

Mom, your husband may not be the heavy-handed parent in your house. If you play that role, is this chapter for you?

Living Translation insightfully translates this verse, "Don't make your children angry by the way you treat them."

When we exasperate our daughters by attempting to control their every move, Colossians 3:21 comes into play: "Fathers, do not embitter your children, or they will become discouraged." To "embitter" means to "overcorrect, provoke, or bring to resentment." "Discouraged" describes what happens when our daughters feel that they always lose. The word literally means "to lose heart."

Heather felt that every disagreement would result in my winning and her losing. She would then "power up" because she expected me to say no to her requests. When I did, she hardened even further; why try if there's no hope of working out a compromise? After many unnecessary battles, I began to choose to lose sometimes. As The Message puts it, "Don't come down too hard on your children or you'll crush their spirits."

I imagine how the prodigal son's dad felt when his son demanded his inheritance early. He knew his son would waste it. But the dad chose to lose that battle. When the son found himself homeless and hungry, perhaps he reflected on his father's grace in that compromise. He knew his father would take him back.

Dads, a battle lost now may allow you to eventually win the war for your daughter's life and soul. Consider these ideas on how to lose, and yet win.

How to Apply Relational Life Preserver 7

1. Realize that every battle need not become a Rubicon.

In ancient times, the boundary between Italy and Gaul was called the Rubicon. When Caesar crossed it with his army in 49 BC, it became an act of war. Today we use the word *rubicon* to describe a point of no return—a line that, once crossed, means irrevocable commitment. We all have our own rubicons with our daughters. If they cross them, we declare war. Many dads and daughters have made every issue a rubicon. One single dad with a teen daughter remarked, "We fought about everything."

Sometimes simple personality differences cause these conflicts. Your garage may reveal your personality type—with 423 bins for nails and screws, each labeled with size and date purchased; 62 shelves for your paint and bug spray; and 94 hooks and hangers on your pegboard for your power and garden tools—everything perfectly displayed just like at Home Depot. Your daughter's room may reveal her personality type, resembling a radiation experiment gone bad. If that's your case, the goal of a clean room may create huge conflicts.

Heather and I butted heads on many issues over which, had we called a truce, life could have been easier. After one unnecessary battle, I asked myself some important questions. I wrote in my journal, "How am I going to respond to this [conflict]? I need to back off. I must still enforce the important rules, but what can I pull away from?" I finally begin to heed James Dobson's counsel, "Pick and choose what is worth fighting for, and settle for something less than perfection on issues that don't really matter."[2]

I began to selectively choose my rubicons. Everything would not become a battle I had to win. I had to save my energy for the crucial issues. Dads, save your best efforts for the critical battles. If you refuse to make a minor issue a major one, you'll have the energy to tackle the big ones when they come. Wisely choose which battles you fight and which hills you're willing to die for.

2. Apply a twofold test to discover your rubicons.

Your battles with your daughter will usually fall into one of two categories: moral/ethical/respect issues and personal preferences. When I realized that many of our battles rose not out of moral areas but from personal preferences, I began to back off.

As you consider your battle lines, ask yourself this key question: "Does this issue compromise a moral or ethical value, or does it simply fall within a personal preference area?" Bruce Narramore provides a list of attitudinal areas you might want to consider as you determine your rubicons. Battles you might be willing to lose include these:

- Increased assertiveness.
- More direct expression of their own opinions about clothes, entertainment, politics, and family activities.
- Increased "forgetfulness" about chores and family responsibilities.
- Complaining about chores and family activities.
- Goofing off or being silly, especially around friends.
- Making some decisions with which parents may disagree— decisions that are legal.
- Keeping secrets from parents.
- Occasional stubbornness.
- Periods of a critical or condemning attitude toward parents or other authorities.

You might add to your list:

- Telephone and television use (within reason).
- A messy room.
- Not wanting to go to church.
- An occasional bad grade.
- Spending money carelessly.
- Some clothing choices.
- Hair color.
- Music choices (check out, however, what your daughter listens to).

On the other hand, Dr. Narramore lists areas on which we shouldn't compromise:

- Chronic irritability and negativism.
- Rebellion or defiance.
- A *don't care* attitude toward parents and all authorities.
- An inability to work cooperatively, even with their peers.
- Frequent depressing or raging outbursts.
- Prolonged angry withdrawal.[3]

I would add the following to this list:

- Sexual involvement.
- Drug involvement.
- Underage drinking.
- Suggestive dress.
- Lying.
- Shoplifting.
- Skipping school or failing classes.
- Running away.

Every dad must make clear to his daughter the consequences of crossing a rubicon. In the negotiable areas, stay flexible.

3. Decide how you will gracefully lose the battles that you've chosen to lose.

One of the toughest choices you will face is to know when to stand your ground and when to give in. If we lose a battle but blow up in the process or make our daughter pay the next time around, we will hurt our relationship. However, if we graciously lose a battle, we build credibility to eventually win the war.

If chores have become a battleground, consider Kevin Lehman's suggestion:

[Adjust your] children's schedules and responsibilities based on their stage in life. If your kids are legitimately busy, cut them some slack. Start taking out the garbage yourself, and help them get through this transition time in their life. If you've raised them right, this won't spoil them, but it will make the adolescent years go a lot more smoothly.[4]

Perhaps a conversation like this with your daughter will help: "We've really disagreed lately about your chores. I know this is a difficult time in your life with [exams, boyfriend breakup, whatever]. How about my taking those chores for the next two weeks to give you a breather? You can get back to doing them on [fix a date]s." Sound risky? Sure. But a simple "give" on your part may open up a "give" on her part.

If your daughter's attire becomes a daily conflict, take a look at your yearbook to remind yourself how you dressed (wild bell-bottoms?) or how long you grew your hair (my dad hated mine). Let your daughter know that you will give her some slack. But draw the line at immodesty. Help her understand how immodest clothing can create problems for boys. I wouldn't always beat her over the head with a Bible verse, though. Sometimes a scientific fact like this may communicate most effectively.

UCLA did a study about how young men interpreted young women's dress. They showed pictures of girls who were dressed very hip, and the girls had told researchers they dressed that way to be fashionable. A majority of the boys, however, said that women who dressed the way were "looking for it" and "advertising" their sexual availability. In short, there was a great disparity between how young women perceived the way they were dressed and how young men interpreted that dress.[5]

Finally, if her room looks like a garbage dump, consider the CTD method that worked quite well for me: CTD = Close the Door.

4. Know how to respond to the Big Three.

Scott Larson points out that "most difficulties with teens fall into one of three categories: dilemmas, crises, or emergencies." Which category an issue falls into will determine the degree of response.

A *dilemma* can be talked through with your daughter, such as finding out that your daughter is dating a boy who's pulling her away from your values. Although very serious, it does not require action from you then and there.

A *crisis*, such as finding out that your sexually active daughter is now pregnant, requires a more immediate response. Writes Larson,

[The situation] now needs your immediate attention, as your daughter is facing significant, life-changing decisions. It is critical for her to be assured immediately that you love her, support her, and will walk through this with her. Her knowing this will help her make rational decisions and give you a better platform to help her with those decisions.

Larson suggests three questions to ask in a crisis:

1. What is the worst possible outcome of this behavior? What if I did nothing?
2. What is my responsibility? Focus on keeping the responsibility on your daughter, and convey that you want to help her through this.
3. What is my objective? Are you trying to avoid embarrassment to yourself or to help her spiritually and emotionally? Ask what would be in your daughter's best interest.[6]

An emergency requires your immediate attention to avoid long-term harm to your daughter. If you overhear your pregnant

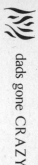

daughter on the phone with an abortion clinic, that is an emergency. This category will require swift and wise decision-making.

Plan how you will respond when your daughter does cross a rubicon. Although you can afford to lose many battles, fight for your daughter if she crosses a rubicon that could bring grave consequences.

Dads, although it may stretch you when you purposely lose a battle, you'll find more peace in your relationship with your daughter when you do. Remember, you parent for the long haul. This means that you keep the future in mind.

Relationship Lifters

- Ask your daughter to write down five nonnegotiable areas where she believes you draw the line. Compare her list with your actual list.
- Pick one negotiable area this week. Tell your daughter that you will give her more flexibility in that area. Intentionally do this each week.
- Ask your daughter where she thinks you both experience the greatest conflict. Discuss practical steps you both can take to compromise.
- Ask your daughter what battles she wants you to lose. Consider losing some.

For Daughters

As I glared at myself in the mirror, a slow, mischievous smile spread across my face. *This will show him,* I thought. I flipped off the bathroom light and slinked down the stairs to leave for church.

My brother and sister loved church and joyfully attended

every Sunday morning. They were also regulars at the barbecues, praise nights, and church potlucks. My mom, an active church member, sang on the worship team every week and headed up several ministry groups. And my dad, of course, was active—he was the *pastor*.

I don't think my mom even looked at me that morning as I stepped into the van and slammed the door shut. As usual, the drive to church was silent. My parents had already endured World War III in their attempts to get me out the door. The fighting, yelling, sulking, and slamming doors had become routine. So now, I had to think of a more creative way to assert my point of view.

My mom drove to church with us kids because my dad had driven in earlier. As we filed out of the van, I made sure to avoid all eye contact with my mom. As the church greeters gave me an enthusiastic "Hi!" I rolled my eyes and went straight to my dad's office. It was the only place I could hide from the "church people" (whom I likened to aliens from some other planet).

My dad strode through the door. I looked up at him, and he stopped and stared.

"Um, hi, Heather."

I detected shock and an I-knew-she'd-do-something tone in his voice.

As I look back on what I put him through (especially on Sunday mornings), I feel sorry for him. I wonder how he's managed to stay out of a straitjacket in a mental ward.

That Sunday, I chose a special "look" (probably to get back at my parents for interrupting my planned fourteen hours of sleep). I was outfitted in black from head to toe: black pants, black shirt, black combat boots. My dyed black hair added to the *Night of the Living Dead*/Marilyn Manson look. And with my fair skin, I looked like an extra on the set of *Dracula*. At that time, I was more into the punk-rock thing—I reserved the scary Goth thing for special occasions that called for specified embarrassment for my parents. In addition to my just-rolled-out-of-bed-to-attend-a-funeral look,

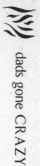
I wore thick, smudged red eyeliner—all around my eyes.

My dad asked, "Heather, are you okay?"

"Yes, I'm fine," I sneered.

My outlandish makeup made me look as if I had been up all night drinking (maybe I had) ... or maybe I just had pinkeye.

I saw my dad's dismay (though he was quite used to my antics and prepared himself for the worst), and I was pleased with myself. I smiled, sweetly said, "Good-bye," and walked into the sanctuary.

In retrospect, I wonder why I did what I did. While my dad most likely felt embarrassed, my rebellious actions only made me look like an idiot. Despite my quest to look as mean and evil as possible, the church members probably weren't fearful; they probably put "poor Heather and her rare eye disease" on the prayer request hot line.

This was one of the many times that I went out of my way to horrify my parents. They had learned to deal with my antics, so I wasn't achieving the desired effect. And every time I tried to "win," I further widened the distance between my father and me. I realize now that in trying to "win" every battle, in many ways I lost more than I gained. Sometimes, it's worth it to just do what you know you're supposed to. That truth didn't penetrate my thick skull for a long time. I became livid when they asked me do things I didn't want to, such as going to church, coming home at a certain hour, changing my outfit, showing up for school, and so on. I kicked and screamed. I sulked. I wanted to win every little battle every time. But my battle strategies didn't work. I learned the hard way that getting my way wasn't always what I really wanted.

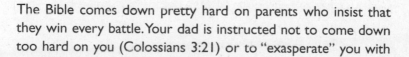

The Bible comes down pretty hard on parents who insist that they win every battle. Your dad is instructed not to come down too hard on you (Colossians 3:21) or to "exasperate" you with nitpicky, unreasonable demands (Ephesians 6:4). Our dads aren't being let off the hook for the way they do their jobs as dads.

But daughters also have a responsibility—to obey. Colossians 3:20 says, "Children, obey your parents in everything." The Bible doesn't say to obey your parents only when you want to, or obey your parents only when they threaten to ground you for the rest of your life. It says, "Obey your parents in *everything*," meaning everything. And obedience is willful; it doesn't include waiting until you get around to it, kicking, screaming, giving attitude, cursing, or threatening (some of my past favorite tactics). We're supposed to be obedient—just because.

I know this can be hard to swallow—doing something just because I'm supposed to has always been hard for me. But as your parents' offspring, that's your job. And you're going to be given a job evaluation from none other than God Himself.

So be willing and cooperative, and try some of these tips to make life less of a war zone.

Appreciate the ways your dad has compromised for you.

I refused to consider the idea of compromise; my dad, on the other hand, mastered it. One time I flew out to Texas to visit a good friend. When my parents picked me up from the airport, I said, "I have a surprise."

Since my dad had become accustomed to my random "surprises," he said, "Okay—let's hear it."

"I got my tongue pierced."

"No, you didn't," he said, chuckling.

"Actually, I did." I stuck out my tongue as proof.

When he looked in the rearview mirror, his eyes grew wide as saucers. Then, an expression I'd seen before crossed his face—the same expression he made when he stepped barefoot on my dog's fresh doo-doo.

"Gross! Put it back! Gross!" he exclaimed.

That was the worst of my reprimand.

While my dad knew that a tongue ring wasn't going to help me get a job or into a good college, he didn't make a fuss about it. I could have done something a whole lot worse, and in the long run, a pierced tongue wasn't anything my dad worried too much about.

In those years, I could have learned a lot from him. I see now the huge compromises he made and how much he let me "win" in order to keep peace between us.

Now, he never relented about his stance on drinking, drugs, and other self-destructive behaviors—understandably—but he looked past the rainbow hair colors, the combat boots, and the piercings.

Think about how much your dad "gives in." Or start noticing if you haven't yet.

Master the fine art of compromise.

Throughout my teenage years, my dad and I fought about pretty much everything. As I've implied, my appearance became a daily battle. Needless to say, my parents didn't appreciate the outfits, and especially not when I wore them to church. They got over how strange the clothes were, but they didn't like how short, tight, and low cut they were. For the most part, my family looked like a "perfect family"—my upright pastor dad, my lovable Southern mom, my role-model Christian brother, and my selfless younger sister. Then there was me, clad in a typical Heather outfit with "I dare you" written all over my face.

One day, however, I tried an experiment. I would have paid for a

Tips for Communicating with Your Dad

- Don't roll your eyes.
- Be respectful.
- Listen more than you speak.
- Sit up straight and look your dad in the eye.
- Don't say "Whatever" (my dad's personal pet peeve).
- Avoid loud sighs or groans.

picture of the look on my parents' faces when I emerged from my room Sunday morning dressed in a light-colored dress looking . . . normal. You would have thought they won the Publishers Clearinghouse Sweep-stakes. "Oh, honey!" they exclaimed. "Oh! You look so nice!"

It was hilarious. I got a kick out of their reaction, and they beamed that their crazy daughter fit into their idea of a somewhat normal child.

See? Strategy changed, but battle won—on both sides.

Try it. Dye your blue hair back to its natural color. Wear something "normal"—it doesn't have to be Abercrombie or a pink frilly dress. Just compromise. Wear the dress your dad likes to church (double points with the parents for the clothes and attending church). It won't kill you, and I'm sure it will show your dad your willingness to compromise.

Talk to your dad about areas where you're willing to let him "win," and areas where you'd like him to let you "win."

To truly win in the end, you've got to give and take. Is it really so important that you wear that three-inch-long skirt to your grandparents' anniversary party? Will it really kill you if you stop listening to the CD with more cursing in the lyrics than actual English words? Do you have to be on the phone with your boyfriend until 4 a.m. every morning (and be at school the next

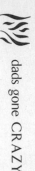

day)? Think about what you're willing to give up. Perhaps when your dad sees your willingness to give, he'll give.

Trade the short skirt for an extended curfew. Trade the crazy hair (if only for a little bit) for more phone time. Try to work out deals with your dad, but do not have an attitude. Don't say, "I'll only do this if you ..." I promise—dads don't go for that. Talk it out with him. Use a nice tone of voice, don't roll your eyes, and don't slouch. Talking with your dad is like a job interview—you want to put your best foot forward. Dad will notice, and who knows? Maybe things will go a lot more smoothly than you think. Remember, it's all give-and-take, so be willing to compromise.

Try The List.

On a piece of paper, make three columns: No, Maybe, and Yes. Let the Yes column represent things you're willing to compromise on; let the Maybe column represent things you might be willing to compromise on; and let the No column represent things you absolutely cannot compromise on. Make sure you write it in pencil. Ask your dad to do one as well.

Now, switch lists. After seeing each other's lists, rewrite your list. Really try to give even another inch—move some of the Nos to Maybes. Now sit down with the revised lists and compare.

First of all, you'll have a better idea of where your dad is coming from. He'll also understand where you're coming from a little bit more.

Second, play "Let's Make A Deal." Begin with the Yes column and work your way through. Be willing to turn some of those Maybes into Yeses. You could switch a No to a Maybe (or a "sometimes.") The most important thing is your willingness to compromise. Ask your dad why some of his Nos are there. He may have some foresight that you didn't think he had.

Relationship Lifters

- Choose one of the things from your list and agree to compromise this week without expecting him to do the same. If you get frustrated, don't use your compromise against him. Remember this is your gift to him.
- Throw away one outfit your dad hates. For me, it was most things I wore, but my dad really hated the skin-tight "painted on" (as he called them) pants and micro-miniskirts. Get rid of just one outfit. Who knows, maybe he'll buy you something to replace it.
- Take your dad shopping (if he'll go). Ask him what outfits he likes. Tell him what outfits you like. Try to reach a happy medium.
- Invite your boyfriend over for dinner with your family. If your parents are uncomfortable with him and all the time you're spending with him, give them a chance to get to know him better. Once they figure out that he's not wanted for murder in thirty-four states, maybe they'll trust you together a little bit more.

Mom to Mom

Nurture your marriage, or you and your husband will have little to give each other. If you don't, your marriage may become much like the two guys in a rowboat that springs a leak. They both furiously bail water from the boat but don't get anywhere because they fail to realize another leak has sprung up.

The emotional drain of managing the situation with your daughter will sap you both, even though you may "bail out" many of the effects of her rebellion. Take stock of your marriage and commit to work as a team. Don't retreat into your corners to lick your wounds. Rather, make time to do what you enjoy doing together. Take a bike ride, watch a movie together, or go for a walk. Charles and I go on a date every Friday. That time has filled our emotional tanks and helped us keep a strong marriage even with the stress that Heather brought.

A Mother's Prayer

Lord, thank You for my husband and for our marriage. Help me not to take them for granted. Guard my heart and my mouth so that I will build up and not tear down those closest to me.

eight

HOPELESS IN THE ER

*Our heavenly father created us a little lower than the
heavenly beings. He knew well that our behavior would often make
us "little better than demons."*[1]
—Dr. John White

*Love never gives up, never loses faith, is always hopeful,
and endures through every circumstance.*
—1 Corinthians 13:7 (NLT)

For Dads

We had just relocated over two thousand miles across the country
to begin a new job and to give Heather a new start. That August she
had attended a youth camp and came back spiritually renewed. I
felt excited about Heather's apparent life-change. I thought, *Maybe
this move will point her in the right direction.* A few weeks later,
though, she shattered our optimism. Her old habits began to
resurface, and I wrote these words in my journal October 10:

> Lord, I feel sick this morning. I see Heather going down, and it
> sickens and scares me. I thought she made a commitment to You,
> but now I'm not sure. Lord, please don't let this happen, for her
> sake. She'll just go back to her life of misery. Please don't let her go
> downhill.

149

We fought an up-and-down battle that fall until one defining moment on December 22 that changed everything.

Sunshine, a rarity for central California in December, greeted us that Friday. I ran some errands that afternoon and came home about two. Sherryl and her sister had gone shopping and the kids were at school, so it was quiet when I walked through the front door of our home. I thought I'd have a few minutes to myself.

In the den I noticed that our well-worn, green La-Z-Boy was on its back as if someone had pushed it over. *That's odd,* I thought, as I pushed it back upright. As I did, I noticed gooey, quarter-inch pink blobs dotting the floor around the chair. "Weird," I said to myself. I tore off a few paper towels, moistened them, and cleaned up the globs.

Suspicious, I climbed the stairs to the second floor where our bedrooms were. I noticed Heather's Chihuahua, Peanut, pacing back and forth in the hall by Heather's room. Something didn't seem right. When he saw me he scampered into Heather's room. I pushed open her slightly ajar door.

Heather was asleep on the bed. I thought, *Oh no. She's skipped school again.*

I stomped over to her bed and demanded, "Heather, get up. Why aren't you in school?"

She didn't move. This time, I sternly yelled, "Heather, get up!"

She still didn't move, and a horrifying thought struck me: *Oh Lord. She's dead.*

My heart began to race. I felt her face to see if it was cold. I was relieved when it felt warm. She was alive. I began to shake her, still unsure why she didn't respond. After I vigorously shook her for more than a minute, she stirred and her eyelids opened to a slit. As soon as they cracked open, her eyes rolled back into her head to reveal only the bloodshot whites of her eyes.

"Heather!" I shouted. "What's wrong? What's wrong?"

She mumbled something. I then sensed that drugs or alcohol

was involved. I knew we had to get her to a hospital fast. At that moment I heard the front door open and Sherryl, her sister, and our youngest daughter walked in.

I screamed, "Sherryl, get up here. Quick!"

She ran upstairs into Heather's room and I mechanically informed her, "Heather has had some drug overdose."

We quickly threw a pair of jeans on Heather and carried her limp body to our SUV. As I floored it for the twenty-minute ride to the hospital, I called 9-1-1 to explain our situation. They some-what calmed my fears because Heather was now semiawake, which they said was a positive sign.

I screeched into the ER turnaround and cut the engine. I jumped out to grab a wheelchair and lifted Heather into it. I wheeled her into the waiting room. When they took her into the ER, they placed her on a gurney. After the nursing staff ascertained her situation, they began IVs.

I stood at a distance as Heather uttered gibberish. I felt disconnected from the whole experience as the commotion of an ER surrounded her brightly lit cubicle. The hushed drone of the nurses discussing their patients . . . the heart monitor's *beep beep beep* . . . the medicinal hospital smell.

I couldn't believe that three days before Christmas, Heather would do such a thing. I felt embarrassed, incensed, disgusted, and worst of all, utterly hopeless. We had shed countless tears and spent thousands of dollars for professional help to give Heather a chance to turn her life around. What did she have to show for it? There she lay in an alcohol-induced stupor, barely having escaped death.

Then a hospital social worker showed up to quench my last embers of hope. "I've seen teens like this," he said. "It doesn't look good. You'd better get her help before she kills herself. These can be complicated situations."

I felt like punching him. These thoughts then crowded my

mind: *How dare you tell us we need to get her help? You don't know what we've done for her.*

As I stood there hopeless, dazed, and broken, I didn't need somebody's trite counsel. I needed hope—hope that this episode would not foreshadow even worse times.

Heather became more lucid but still seemed to speak out of her head. For thirty minutes she kept slurring, "Dad, I'll . . . I'll . . . I'll make you, you proud. I pr— pr—promise. I'll do b— better. I'll change."

Mom's Tip

Mom, you may need to serve as the primary "hope giver" in your family if your husband can't. If so, ask God to continually infuse you with His hope.

In my hopelessness I muttered under my breath, "Yeah. You'll make me proud. Just like you've made me proud right now. And just like you've made me proud the last five years."

I never felt more hopeless than I did at that point. I'm convinced, though, that God engineered that circumstance to give Heather one last chance to change. Although despondency engulfed me, that moment became a "hinge of hope" upon which God began to move her life in a new direction.

From that point, Heather began her transformation. The horror and embarrassment of that event paved the way for her return. That day I realized that even the worst experience may become the catalyst to change a person's direction.

⚜

The hope that fills the pages of Scripture has enabled Christians throughout history to face insurmountable obstacles with dignity, courage, and faithfulness. The Greek word for "hope" appears eighty-seven times in the New Testament. The biblical writers usually used it to convey something concrete we can cling to. It means that we must keep our confidence in God that He will use the difficult circumstances to change our daughters.

Spiritual giants of the Bible often wrote about this. The apostle Paul wrote, "May the God of hope fill you with all joy and peace as you trust in him, so that you may overflow with hope by the power of the Holy Spirit" (Romans 15:13). The psalmists learned to fight hopelessness during difficult times when they penned, "Why am I discouraged? Why so sad? I will put my hope in God!" (Psalm 42:5 NLT).

The prophet Jeremiah experienced the power of hope. An entire book of the Bible, Lamentations, records his heartbreak at Israel's rebellion. Yet, he revealed his hope in these words:

> I will never forget this awful time, as I grieve over my loss. Yet I still dare to hope when I remember this: The unfailing love of the LORD never ends! By his mercies we have been kept from complete destruction. Great is his faithfulness; his mercies begin afresh each day. I say to myself, "The LORD is my inheritance; therefore, I will hope in him!" (Lamentations 3:20–24 NLT)

Dads, if you feel hopeless, be encouraged. Some of the strongest Christians who have ever lived have felt the same way. Yet they refused to stay at the bottom because they *learned* to hope. We naturally respond to disappointment with discouragement. We can't reverse this negative thinking with simple platitudes and "positive thinking." Rather, hope grows when we burrow deep into God's Word, trusting that he will sustain us.

How to Apply Relational Life Preserver 8

1. Don't bottle your feelings.

Most men find it difficult to express emotions that reveal their vulnerability, such as grief. We tend to bottle our emotions because culture expects men not to cry. Since we play the role as provider, protector, and fixer, when our daughters rebel, it implies we failed our jobs. We think grief could further stifle our ability to be strong dads. So, we just suck it up, get superbusy, or we throw ourselves into a task.

We can postpone this emotion only so long. If we stuff it, it may show up through unhealthy anger, workaholism, or sexual compromise. If we don't let ourselves feel our pain, our hearts can also become callused to our daughters. We must grieve over the hurt we experience.

It's important that we go against society's expectations about us. We must feel and express our grief because God gives us tears for a purpose. Grieving doesn't mean that we lose hope; rather, it's a prelude to it. It means that we honestly face our disappointments, experience grief's cleansing effects, and turn our hope back to God.

Because I grieve internally, I needed an outlet to release my emotions. Journaling gave me that outlet. When I wrote my feelings, tears came more easily. They helped wash away my sorrow. Max Lucado says, " When words are most empty, tears are most apt."[2]

Allow the Lord to help you release your pain through tears. Try journaling. Or, find a safe friend. Consider an appointment with a counselor. Whatever you do, guard against frenzied activity to avoid tears.

2. Never give up hope.

S. Rutherford McDill captures the essence of hope when he writes the following:

The kind of hope you need is that which drives [you] to hang in there in the face of no evidence that anything is working—at least not yet. This kind of hope is the muscle behind the absence of gratitude or effects—at least for now. This hope is the wind that keeps you moving forward, looking for better days ahead in the face of nothing but bad. This hope drives and sustains and can be at the core of a positive-outcome, self-fulfilling prophecy.[3]

When I wanted to give up, God reminded me that the prodigal son's father never did. Every day he scanned the horizon to look for his son. He modeled God's relentless pursuit of us even when we rebel. God never gives up on us. As long as our daughters are alive, we must not give up on them.

God also nudged me to not give up through the story of the shepherd who left the ninety-nine to find the one lost sheep. One psychologist reminded me that Heather saw herself as an angry sheep and me as the shepherd. I couldn't stop going after

---

SIX SIMPLE STEPS FOR EFFECTIVE JOURNALING

1. Get a notebook.
2. Set a consistent time in a quiet place.
3. Make a commitment to stick with it on a daily or weekly basis.
4. Date each entry.
5. Write from feeling, not from fact. Don't just record what happened in your life. Write down how your experiences affected your heart and emotions.
6. Periodically review your entries to discover spiritual trends in your life.

Since women tend to express feelings more easily than men, you will probably process your pain better than your husband. Pray that God will give him the desire and ability to work through his painful emotions.

her because a good shepherd always goes after the strays. If he loses hope, the strays will die.

In my darkest moments, a glimmer of hope shone through. The day after I wrote in my journal, "I'm at the end of my rope," Heather got sick. The next day I wrote, "Last night she crawled up in bed with us ... she also let me pray for her." The Lord encouraged me through that simple act. He will do the same for you. I even found hope in the law of averages. One survey of thirty-five thousand parents found that only 15 percent of rebellious children continue to reject their parents' values after adolescence.[4] Chances are, your daughter will return.

Remember, though, that sustained optimism lies not in self-effort, but in applying the next point, for genuine hope always flows out of an intimate relationship with God.

3. Draw near to God.

Sherryl and I often asked God why Heather went south. Our other two kids didn't cause us problems. So why her? Job wrote an entire book of the Bible about the "Why, God?" question. Although God never directly answered him, Job didn't turn his back on God.

When our daughters rebel, it's okay to ask "Why?" sometimes, but often, as with Job, God won't answer us. If we don't get an answer or see change, we must cling to Him no matter what. In retrospect, I realized that God used those difficult times to soften my rough edges and create character in me.

When life seems gloomiest, cling to God as did Paul and Silas after they healed a demon-possessed slave girl (Acts 16). This girl made money for her owners with her fortunetelling ability until God healed her. As a result, Paul and Silas ended up in a dark, dank jail. Yet even when the situation seemed darkest, they clung to hope. The placed their trust in God, even though they didn't understand His plan.

Rebellious children come from even the best families. Larry Crabb dealt with a rebellious son. After years of struggle, Dr. Crabb learned this insight, which brought him much healing.

> Something became clear. There were no formulas. There were no right strategies with guaranteed outcomes. There was only God. Would I trust him and rely on his name (not as a new plan to get what I wanted)? Would I simply hold his hand, trust his heart, and move into darkness with no purpose other than to reflect something of Christ? Only deep darkness helped me to fear God more than confusion.[5]

Ron Mehl, before a long battle with leukemia took his life, wrote these words about the importance of a healthy relationship with God during dark times:

> When the darkness comes into our lives, when light seems to vanish and we begin to feel as though the sun will never again break the heaviness of our night, *that* is the time to "trust in the name of the Lord." That is the time to rely on our God and wait for Him. Those who scramble around trying to manufacture their own light and comfort, apart from God, will only find hurt and sorrow at the end of the trail.[6]

4. Persist in prayer.

My wife and I have enjoyed visits to a few lighthouses scattered along the Pacific coast. Stories about brave lighthouse keepers who kept the lights going under horrendous circumstances stir the emotions. When the seas raged, those lights gave the only bearings of safety for captains and their ships in the middle of storms.

When our daughters embroil themselves in life's storms, we're tempted to "turn out the light." After all, they've earned their just rewards, right?

Dads, don't yield to that temptation. Even if our daughters turn their backs on us, they will look to see if we still offer a beacon of hope and open arms. If we turn off the light and slam the door in their faces, we may destroy the last hope for their return by leaving them with no bearings to steer by. Keep the door open and the light on. Pray that you will remain that beacon of safety.

Although the Bible doesn't record the prodigal son's father praying, I know that he must have. His prayers kept his heart hopeful and his arms open. Besides the obvious need to pray for our daughters to turn back to God, consider these topics upon which to focus your prayer.

That you won't lose hope. I wrote in my journal January 31, 2000, "Lord, give me the faith to believe you." I needed God to infuse faith so I wouldn't lose hope.

That your daughter will hit the bottom with minimum long-term damage. I often asked God to break Heather's stubborn will and protect her from choices with serious consequences. This need became apparent after I received this letter from Heather.

> As I have told you before, the only way I will learn is if I hit rock bottom. If it takes me prostituting on the streets to make money for crack, then so be it. If I shoot so much heroin that I O.D. and die, that's my fate. . . . The only way that I will ever change is when my pride has left me, and I'm down on my knees begging for forgiveness. And that will happen no time in the future. The fight won't come out of me. I won't let it.

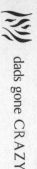

I'm convinced that Heather's alcohol overdose was a direct answer to my prayer.

That you will pray even if you don't know what to pray for. One writer described this kind of prayer after a whale watch in Cape Cod Bay.

The naturalist pointed out two whales that appeared to be floating dead in the water side by side. She explained that the whales were logging, a term for the way whales sleep. Whales sleep in groups for twenty-minute intervals because they can allow only half of their brains to sleep at a time. Otherwise, they would forget to breathe, and drown. Instantly I made a connection with the prayer life of parents. When our children "forget to breathe"—that is, when they shut down all common sense and neglect the basics of their spiritual upbringing—we parents can intercede and function like the other half of their spiritual brains, preventing them from drowning in their rebellion. We can keep the Holy Spirit working actively in their lives.[7]

That other prayer warriors will come alongside you. God brought a woman, Kathy, into our lives who prayed for Heather like no one else. She wrote me a letter after Heather changed, a portion of which describes the power of a prayer warrior and the hope she gave us.

The burden to pray for Heather intensified to the point that I would often be awakened in the middle of the night with a tremendous sense of urgency to pray for her. Sometimes it was almost a physical sense of pain or pressure, often accompanied by tears, that wouldn't lift for long periods of time. I felt prompted to pray for Heather's safety, for her to be caught when she was disobedient to her parents, for her to be convicted of her rebellion, for her to come to the end of herself, and for her to recognize the emptiness of a self-governed life without Christ.

Kathy's prayers came true.

Lastly, there's a story told by Tony Campolo about his pastor, who in one of his rousing sermons stood before the congregation shouting, "It's Friday—but Sunday's comin'!"

The pastor repeated those words over and over until the congregation began chanting them with him. "It's Friday—but Sunday's comin'. It's Friday—but Sunday's comin'." Slow to catch on but excited once they did, these people felt the presence of the Living Hope. They felt the reassurance of Jesus's power to conquer death. The animated pastor imprinted on their hearts the message that Christ will not leave us or forsake us. As you navigate the darkness, listen for Jesus calling your name. He wants you to know that He is there. He will reassure you of His steadfast love. Sunday's comin'.[8]

Dads, hang in there. Your Sunday may come sooner that you think.

Relationship Lifters

- Ask your daughter how you can pray for her. Write down what she says, and pray those requests. If she won't tell you, privately ask God to open her heart so that at some point she will.
- Purchase an inexpensive notebook and try journaling for the next five days. If you find it helps, try it another five days.
- This week, write a letter of hope to your daughter. List all the positives you see in her and describe how you envision her landing well.

For Daughters

> I don't remember anything. . . . It's what, December 22 or 23, a
> few days 'til Christmas, and I don't even know if it's 9:05 a.m. or
> p.m. . . . But I'm *alive* . . .
> —Entry in Heather's journal

Beep . . . Beep . . . Beep . . .
Where am I? . . .

As my head began to fall forward, I jolted upright. Sleeping in
class . . . again. I blinked my eyes a few times and slumped back in
my seat.

I checked the clock. Nope. Still plenty of time left until class
was over. I folded my arms and laid my head back down on the
desk. I was stuck in senior English class—or as it really should
have been called, "nap time."

"Hey . . . Heather!" one of my classmates whispered.

I slowly righted myself and stretched. I turned my head to see
what he wanted. Only a few months earlier, my life had dramatically changed. My family had moved from a booming suburban
area outside of Atlanta to a tiny town where the almond orchards
outnumbered the residents.

When they told me we were moving to California, visions of
palm-tree-lined streets, aqua waves crashing on an ivory beach,
and year-round tropical weather filled my mind. But they don't tell
you everything about California. The only palm trees in this town
were on a palm tree farm. Instead of beaches, there were seas of
dying, yellowed grass. Instead of herds of blonde people, we had
herds of . . . cows. This was not California as I had pictured it. This
was a Central Valley town with a population of ten thousand. I
was angry . . . and miserable. I hated the place, I hated the people,
I hated the school—I hated everything. And when I was miserable, I made everyone around me miserable.

Before the move, I had (for the most part) stopped the drugs, and I kind of mellowed out. But my hatred and bitterness were evident in everything I said and did, especially in my home life. My dad tried everything to make my life easier, even buying me a car. But I wouldn't have it. I was unhappy, bitter, and alone. I felt hopeless. So I returned to the thing that I'd used to dull the pain in the past—alcohol.

"Yeah?" I said sleepily as I rubbed my eyes.

"Do you want to come with us?"

"Where?"

"We're going over to Jon's for some drinks. Let's get out of here."

I think everybody at that school figured I was up for almost anything, including getting smashed at 10 a.m. I regularly skipped class or didn't even show up, and stories about my partying had already been circulating around the school. In the middle of English class, without a word, we gathered our book bags and walked out the door.

It was a beautiful day. The sun shone brightly in the cloudless blue sky, and the crisp December air invigorated me as I left school. We walked off the campus and down the street a few blocks to a house. One of the guys crawled inside his bedroom window to unlock the front door.

Once inside, I sat back on the couch and looked at the carefully decorated Christmas tree and the stockings hanging above the fireplace. I thought, *The happiest time of the year . . . right.*

A glass of vodka shoved in my face brought me back to reality.

"Merry Christmas!" we toasted. We clanked glasses. I began to gulp.

The last thing I remember was the burning liquid running down my throat and the all-too-familiar smell of vodka.

Beep . . . beep . . . beep.

What is that stupid noise? I wondered. My head felt as if it was in a vise that kept tightening as the room spun.

162

I squinted up at the fluorescent lights . . . and finally made out white ceiling tiles. I noticed white squares stuck to my chest with wiring coming from them. I blinked a few times, then looked down at the IVs coming from each arm. I followed the tubing up to the dripping bag of saline. My eyes focused beyond the tubing and I saw my parents looking at me fearfully, with a sense of urgency and hopelessness in their eyes.

I still wasn't thinking clearly enough to figure out what was going on. "Where . . . What am . . . What is this?" I slurred.

I still remember the hurt and sadness on my mom's face, and the way she held my limp hand.

"You got alcohol poisoning and almost died," said my dad mechanically.

I began my drunken declaration. "I won't do it again. I promise. I'll make you proud. I promise . . . I'll make you proud. I'll make you proud . . ."

I don't remember the ride home from the hospital a few hours later or being carried to my bed and passing out.

I spent Christmas break recovering from the worst hangover of my life. I was able to piece together the events of that day after I'd questioned my parents and talked to the guys I had been with.

After drinking so much liquor on an empty stomach (I'm a lightweight at 115), I started puking at Jon's house. I ran to his bathroom and vomited all over everything—the sink, the toilet, the floor. They cleaned up that bathroom just in time for me to wander to the other bathroom and start puking all over it. After some time elapsed (I still don't *really* know what happened), they drove me to my house, making a few vomit-on-the-side-of-the-road stops along the way. Somehow I'd managed to crawl upstairs to my room and pass out on the bed. My parents had rushed me to the ER.

A few things stood out to me as I reflected back on this experience. First, about those "friends." I asked myself, *What kind of friends just drop you off at your house when you're obviously very, very sick?* I realized they were looking out only for themselves and were more concerned with covering their butts than with making sure I was all right.

Secondly, while my "friends" just left me at my house, it was my dad who carried me to his car and rushed me to the ER. I was eighteen years old; he could have easily thrown me out of the house for good. However, he gave me yet another chance that I didn't deserve. Even when I gave him no reason at all to hope I would ever change for the better, he refused to give up on me. He never lost hope.

Even though I'd horrified him in front of visiting family and had ruined my family's entire Christmas, he still loved me and held onto our relationship, no matter how hard it was for him. He never quit praying that I'd be okay one day.

At this point in your life, maybe you could care less if your dad is a part of your life. You may see him as some tyrant who's just trying to make your life difficult. But look deeper. My dad told me not to drink—because he knew that alcohol could kill me, not because he wanted to spoil my fun. He told me not to have sex— to protect me from STDs, pregnancy, and selfish guys, not to impose his power on me. He told me not to do drugs—so I wouldn't become an addict on the street or end up like Ozzy Osbourne by the age of thirty. I was too wrapped up in myself to realize that he just wanted me to be happy and that I needed him.

He didn't spend tens of thousands of dollars on rehabs and counselors, waiting up for me countless nights, and screw my windows shut because he had nothing better to do. He did it because he loved me and because he still hoped that we could renew our relationship. It was the only way he knew to try to save me from myself.

I can't say that about my "friends." I placed more value on my relationships with those so-called friends than I did on my relationship with my dad. As soon as I quit using drugs and partying, I hardly saw them anymore. And the boyfriends were temporary. When everything was against me, my dad was always the one who was there for me, standing behind me, fighting for me, and supporting me.

A famous man in the Bible named Paul spent a great deal of his later life in jail. Upon converting from being a crusader against Christianity to a believer, Paul dedicated his life to Jesus. His new courageous crusade for Christ offended the power players of the day. He was persecuted, beaten, and thrown in jail more times than he could probably count. But he still wrote of hope: "We also rejoice in our sufferings, because we know that suffering produces perseverance; perseverance, character; and character, hope. And hope does not disappoint us" (Romans 5:3–4).

You may not care about your relationship with your dad—you may even have given up hope of having a relationship with him. Don't! Don't give up. Don't push your father out of your life . . . keep giving the relationship a chance. Give him some reason to hold on to hope that things will get better. Keep hope alive by using these few ideas.

Don't lose the man in your life.

As I did some research for this book, I found a Web site called *Imissmydad.com*. It's a collection of hundreds of e-mail messages from people of all ages who've lost their fathers in various ways. The e-mail that follows stood out to me.

Dad, I miss you so much, words can't explain the emptiness I feel inside because you are gone. You left me so suddenly, I had no time to even think about what my life would be like without you in it. You and I were so excited about my wedding, now I have to go on with the biggest day of my life without you there, how will I ever make it through. I know you will be with me, always in my heart.

I have no regrets when it comes to our relationship, I just have a lot of wishes. We were just about as close as a father and daughter could be. I told you I loved you all the time, I just wish I could still tell you, and you could hear me. You were the best father anyone could ask for. I am the person I am today because of you, and all that you taught me. I always thought of you as just my Dad, never taking into account what an extraordinary person you were. I just wish I had realized all the wonderful things about you when you were here. We just don't think of those things, we often take them for granted.

I'd give anything to go back to the day before you died, so I would not have treated it as just an ordinary day, I would have treated it as if it were my last day with you. Which is how I should have treated everyday I had with you. I don't know how I will go on, it has been four months, and I miss you more and more everyday. I have so much to tell you and so much to share. When will the tears dry up, and the pain go away. Just please know how much I love you and always will. You will always be the only true love in my life. I Love You!

Perhaps this example sounds off the subject and extreme, but it's not. Why would we, who have our fathers, trash them when so many other kids—teens whose fathers have died—would give anything for one more day with them? It's so easy to become estranged from your father. But you don't want to miss out on him at these incredible milestones in your life—he needs to be there. So don't keep pushing him out by doing stupid things that could destroy hope for a renewed relationship. You may never know how much he means to you until it's too late.

Don't mortally wound the relationship.

Growing up, I didn't care about my dad—and I let him know it. I thought he wanted to mold me into the perfect Christian daughter, meaning I never left the house without my Bible, I had a wardrobe consisting of only ankle-length pleated skirts and turtlenecks, and I held convictions such as *I won't date until I'm thirty.* That's not what he wanted at all. But because I assumed the worst about him, I came to a point when I gave up all hope of our ever getting along or seeing eye to eye on anything—and I just quit the relationship.

I can't imagine where I'd be now without my dad. I'm so glad he's alive and not dead. I need him for so many things. To have him absent from my life would have left a gaping hole in my heart. I can't tell you the joy he's brought me. Don't cheat yourself out of it! Your dad is special—don't throw out the relationship by doing something stupid to permanently alienate him. Be strong enough to get through it. You'll one day see how getting along was worth it.

You don't want to be left with regrets. Get to know him. Maybe you don't get it now (I didn't), but I promise you—when your dad becomes one of your best friends and the man you love and respect most in this world, you will understand how much you need him.

And now, another e-mail from someone named Jamie about poignant last regrets:

> I let myself find other excuses, and managed to exclude him from the many aspects of my life.
> And now he's gone.
> I thought a lifetime of missed opportunities between us would be put to rest once and for all. That the finality of it would have a comforting peace. But like two stubborn people on a see-saw, neither moving, when one is suddenly gone, all that pain and frustration tumbles down to the heavier side. I never imagined

this loss would hurt so badly. That my regret would amount to so much sadness and heartfelt pain. That the man, who growing up, never failed to hug me and tell me he loved me and was proud of every little thing I did—would be gone, and I would feel so ashamed for not spending enough time with him, and including him in my life.

My dad was a great man. He never enjoyed a life as richly as he deserved. But he loved unselfishly. Expecting nothing in return. He gave what he could, and that was always enough. He helped so many people that simply needed a friend. In death, I wish I had been a better friend to him. This is my lasting regret.

I miss you dad. I hope you know how much I love you. Jamie[9]

Don't wound the relationship with your dad. You don't want to have a lasting regret like Jamie's.

Relationship Lifters

- Get to know this guy. Ask your dad about his teenage years. Ask him what his relationship was like with his dad. Ask him what he was interested in, what music he listened to, what crazy things he did. Take the time to simply get to know him. Old people have some pretty cool stuff to talk about.
- Think *first*, then act. If you finding yourself getting really angry, wait to cool down before you talk to him. Ask for a "time out" or time by yourself. This can keep things from escalating.
- Stretch. Don't be afraid to let him have the last word.
- Make a list of all the reasons you want to keep your dad in your life. When you're tempted to just give up, go over your list. It should give you that something you need to keep trying.

Mom to Mom

Hold on to hope.

As long as I can remember I longed to be a mother. Years before I became pregnant with Heather, I prayed for my future child and readied myself to be the best mother I could when that day came.

Her toddler years proved a bit testy, but she became more manageable as she approached the pre-K years. Her grade-school years were much like a pilot's smooth ride once he reaches his cruising altitude.

But as you've read, then she hit thirteen. Her unexpected nosedive made me often cry, "Mayday! MayDay!" to God, to Charles, and to my closest friends. As the plunging darkness continued to overtake me, I wondered if I had lost hope. Her steep descent lasted so long that several times I prayed that I would live long enough to see Heather return to God.

One day I came across a verse in Romans that deeply touched my heart. I memorized it, and for months I quoted it and prayed it on behalf of Heather. "May the God of hope fill you with all joy and peace as you trust in him, so that you may overflow with hope by the power of the Holy Spirit" (Romans 15:13 NIV).

A faith transfusion started to occur, and I began to ask the God of hope to replace my hopelessness with His hope by the power of His Holy Spirit. Mom, cling to the hope of God's word. Allow the Holy Spirit to infuse His hope into your heart.

A Mother's Prayer

O Lord, the God of hope,
I ask You to fill me with joy and peace
as I trust completely in You.
Replace my hopeless feelings with
hopeful ones. Fill my heart
and my thoughts to overflowing
with Your hope.

nine

THE PRODIGAL RETURNS

*They don't come home one day smelling like a pigpen
and get up the next morning smelling like a rose—doing
everything the way you'd like.*[1]
—A mom with a prodigal

For Dads

After the ER discharged Heather we brought her home, tucked her
into bed, and brought her milk and cookies. Then an amazing
transformation took place almost overnight. After a long nap she
got up and asked to speak to us. We settled into our cushy den
couch and listened. With a broken heart she apologized for every
sin she had committed the past five years. As she finished her teary
two-hour confession, she blessed our hearts with these godly
promises.

> Dad and Mom, I've been so wrong. I now realize that when you
> daily told me, "One day you'll thank us for everything we did for
> you," I should have been thankful. You were right. Everything you
> said and did deserves my thanks. Thank you for all those curfews,
> groundings, and lectures. The Bible says to honor your parents. I
> now promise to set a good example for my brother and sister on
> how best to honor you. From this point, I will never dispute your
> word again.

171

I will throw away all my punk-rock CDs and set my radio to a wholesome classical station. I will do something meaningful with my life by volunteering in the nursery at church each Sunday and Wednesday night. I will memorize a Bible verse during my daily one-hour quiet time.

I will let you and Mom go through my closet to remove those disgusting, immodest clothes. I'll get a job at the Christian bookstore to earn my own money to buy new clothes that I'll let you pick out. After all, Dad, as you often told me, I need to show responsibility.

I will go to bed at ten o'clock each night and will set my curfew on weekends to 10:30 p.m.—not 10:31, but 10:30 exactly. I will date only guys who plan to become missionaries to the Amazon. I will let you interview them and run a background check on them before I go on a date. And then we will attend only gospel concerts in churches that feature organ and violin, no drums or electric guitars. The only man I will ever kiss again will be my future husband. I will not kiss him until our wedding ceremony.

I will take out the trash and empty the dishwasher every day without being asked. I will never leave a dirty towel on the bathroom floor again. I will make up my bed every day, complete with comforter and pillow shams in place.

I will limit my telephone time to from 8:00–8:30 each night, but only after I've finished my homework, laid out my clothes for the next day, and brushed and flossed my teeth. I promise to make straight As and will join the Girl Scouts, 4-H, and Future Homemakers of America. Then I will become a missionary to the unreached people groups in New Guinea.

I'm a brand new me.

From that point forward, peace ruled our home. It was the picture-perfect prodigal return. Heather never disobeyed us again. We lived happily every after.

If you believe what I just wrote, please call 1-800-G-U-L-L-I-B-L-E for a great deal on some investment property in the Arizona desert.

✦━✦

Contrary to my make-believe description, Heather's return to our family felt more like a family of porcupines trying to snuggle. Occasionally we saw quick, dramatic changes. Other times it felt like two steps forward, three steps back. Now, several years later, we still butt heads.

Mom's Tip

Mom, honestly evaluate your expectation for your daughter's return. If it's unrealistic, ask God to help you make it more realistic.

Most parents won't experience dramatic, instant transformations of prodigals and we didn't with Heather. I hoped for a prodigal-son-type return, complete with a once-for-all repentant heart. It didn't happen. Don't be alarmed if your daughter's return comes slowly. Consider these ways, however, to soften your daughter's reentry into your family.

HOW TO APPLY RELATIONAL LIFE PRESERVER 9

1. Stay realistic about what a return will look like.

Every dad dreams that his daughter will return with a broken and repentant heart like that of the prodigal son. However, Jesus doesn't tell us what happened in the months after that son returned. If this story is more than a parable, a view some scholars hold, then perfect peace didn't follow. The son's penchant to wander probably didn't evaporate on the day he returned. And he gave the father no guarantee that he would not fall back into some

173

of his ways. After I realized this, I became more realistic about Heather's return.

Your daughter may return in dramatic fashion. Heather didn't. Her return was a process. She made great strides when she attended an intensive nine-month spiritual growth school. That experience immersed her in Bible study, fellowship with other Christians, and character training in an insulated environment (no TV, movies, or radio). A few months after this experience though, her fire for God waned.

Our friend, Kathy, who had prayed for Heather for five years, calls the good times "spiritual honeymoons with God," that lead us to publicly renew our commitment to God. Sadly, the emotional impact often dims in the weeks that follow. You may find the same true for your daughter after a deeply spiritual experience or a crisis.

Expect those experiences, and allow time for changes to stick. Often we didn't see progress except in retrospect. Your relationship with your daughter may happen so gradually that suddenly one day you may realize how much things have improved. Be patient, and let time do its work.

2. Create an atmosphere of forgiveness in your home.

The Bible often commands us to forgive those who hurt us. The apostle Paul captured the essence of forgiveness when he wrote Colossians 3:13: "Forgive as the Lord forgave you." Forgiveness, rightly understood and applied, will bring great healing to your relationship with your daughter.

Just as her return will take time, so will genuine forgiveness. Don't expect a nice, neat, linear experience. We can't switch on a once-for-all forgiveness button. The deeper the hurt, the longer it takes to fully forgive. I forgave (and still forgive) Heather over and over again.

True forgiveness does not diminish the seriousness of your

daughter's rebellion, nor does it deny your feelings. Rather, it can—

- Initiate a thaw in the relationship.
- Keep you from seeing your daughter as the enemy.
- Help you surrender your desire to get even with your daughter.
- Remove the demand for ironclad guarantees that her old behavior won't return.
- Break the temptation to keep score.
- Free you from emotionally tying yourself to your daughter's ups and downs.
- Enable you to pray for your daughter more easily.
- Remind you of God's grace.

Should you wait for your daughter to ask for forgiveness before you offer it? Ideally she would do that, but she may not. When we refuse to forgive, we chain our hearts to our daughters' offenses. We must break those chains of unforgiveness even without her repentance.

Even the prodigal son's dad extended forgiveness before his son repented. His gifts conveyed comprehensive forgiveness. Was it easy for him? Probably not. We don't know the dad's thoughts and feelings while his son was gone. Like most dads, though, he must have struggled to forgive.

It might be appropriate to verbalize our forgiveness to our daughter. Other times it won't be. Words may become catalysts for forgiveness, but in themselves they don't embody it. Genuine forgiveness happens deep within our hearts.

Perhaps a letter will help you begin to forgive. At the top of a piece of paper write, "Dear Daughter." Under that write, "I forgive you for—" and complete the sentence with the first thought that comes to mind. With each new thought, write, "I forgive you

> ### *Mom's Tip*
>
> If your husband struggles to forgive your daughter, perhaps you need to model how to forgive. Gently, without nagging, tell your husband how you learned to forgive.

for—" and complete the sentence. Do this as long as the hurts come to mind. Your list may end up short or long. It doesn't matter, as long as you stay honest with yourself. After no other thoughts come to mind, place an empty chair in front of you and visualize your daughter in it. Read your list aloud, and imagine your daughter accepting your forgiveness with verbal and nonverbal responses. After you read the list, don't show it to anyone; destroy it.

Dads, you and I must choose whether or not to forgive. It will prove difficult. However, you can never calculate the cost of not forgiving. Woodrow Kroll, teacher and author with *Back to the Bible,* received a letter from a mother whose daughter rebelled years earlier. In that letter she captured the difficulty to forgive and the choice we must make to forgive.

> Our daughter did come home. As well as I can know my heart, I have forgiven her fully. But through the nearly twenty years that have followed, her father's hurt still lingers. And her brother continues to hold her rebellious teen years against her. Forgiveness and acceptance of the returning prodigal does not come easy.[2]

Forgiveness will not guarantee a restored relationship, because restoration takes effort from both of you. Forgiveness, however, is unilateral. You can choose it regardless of her response. When you do, the next step becomes possible.

3. See your daughter through new eyes.

World-renowned communication expert Deborah Tannen

points out that every person has two great emotional needs—and they are often in conflict. "One is the need to be connected to others in relationship, and the other is the need to be an individual who is not controlled by others."[3]

Because our daughters feel those needs, we must begin to see them through new eyes as they mature. Our daughters will never revert to pigtailed, jump-in-Daddy's-lap little girls. To see them and treat them as adults takes concerted effort.

When we were writing this book, Heather lived with us. As a result, I still felt tempted to treat her as I did when she was a teen by "telling" more than "suggesting." When we planned to sell her blue car, I made an effort to change my approach. Before, I would have said, "Heather, go clean up your car so we can sell it." But because I began to see her through new eyes I suggested, "Heather, it would be great if you could get your car cleaned up so we could sell it. I'd like to advertise it in the paper this weekend."

Dad, as your daughter begins to come back into your life and family, ask God to give you a new set of eyes. If you can see your daughter as more grown-up, it will help her become appropriately responsive to you.

Karen, a seventeen-year-old from Minneapolis, wrote a letter to her father that captures the attitude we need.

Dear Daddy, I hope you won't be mad at me, but I need to tell you to back off (there's no other way I can say it). I love you, and you are the greatest dad in the world, but I am not a little girl anymore. You need to let me go. I used to think it was neat when you would say how you hate it that I was growing up, but now I don't think it is. I want you to know that, whether you like it or not, I am growing up, and I am becoming a woman. It's now up to me to decide what I do, what I wear, who I date, and how I spend my time. If you don't let me or try to stop me, I'll do it anyway. I don't mean to hurt you, but I'm almost eighteen and then I really am on my own (legally). So, Dad, please let me go![4]

4. Become more of a mentor figure than a parent figure.

Fathering at this stage becomes more like mentoring. A parent figure sets the agenda for the child. A mentor figure allows his mentoree to set the agenda and what she wants to accomplish.

Discern what your daughter wants in life and be there with guidance, when she asks. Guard against the temptation to pry. If she wants to talk, then talk. If she doesn't, don't force the issue (unless the issue is of a life-threatening nature). Let her choose. You may not want to know everything she did in her rebellious times. As we wrote this book together, Heather told me some hair-raising choices she made that I couldn't have handled earlier. I'm glad I didn't press to discover everything she did. (Even as I rewrite my section of this chapter based on Heather's editorial comments, I smile as I read what she wrote in the margin. Next to "I'm glad I didn't press to discover everything she did," she wrote, "Yes, you are.")

Although I'm still learning how to mentor her, when I made this subtle shift, our relationship took a step forward.

5. Respect your daughter's differing views.

Although our relationship is stronger than ever, Heather and I still disagree on many issues. One day as we watched the news she remarked that she wasn't going to vote for a certain candidate for president—the obvious good choice, as far as I was concerned. It ticked me off, but her comment forced me to realize that I must honor her political views.

Many of Heather's music choices befuddle me. When I drive her car and one of her CDs begins to play, if I listen very long I become confused and disoriented and wonder, *Is that music?* I'm sure my classical music gets on her nerves as well. Although I may not like the style or lyrics of her music, she knows I won't make an issue of it. If I've done a good job teaching her how to make wise choices, I must trust her to choose wisely.

I also hold a high standard for the movies I see. In the last twenty-five years I've watched only one R-rated movie at the theater—and it was *The Passion of the Christ*. Heather doesn't hold the same standard. I used to make this a big issue, but now I don't. She knows what I believe and respects my convictions.

Dads, this short list of our differences represents a small part of our conflicting views. You and your daughter could make your own list. Whatever lands on that list, realize that your daughter does not want you to put down her values that differ from yours. You can respect her views, however, without agreeing with them. As you learn to ease up, God will add new life to your relationship.

6. Expect mixed emotions.

Even after Heather began her return to us and to God, sometimes she said or did something that emotionally felt like a metal bristle brush scraped across a scab. I had forgiven her and I felt joy at the positive steps I saw in her. At the same time, though, fear and anger clashed with those good feelings. It felt like emotional schizophrenia. I could feel elated at her softened spirit toward us, but in the next minute I'd feel skeptical that it wouldn't last long or angry for the hurt she had caused.

Brendan O'Rourke and DeEtte Sauer describe this experience as "reunion grief." They write,

> The term refers to the strange tendency of humans to have difficulty receiving the thing they have most longed for, but learned to live without." For example, "The adult child of the recovering alcoholic is both pleased to see his parent stop drinking and enraged that it took so long. Accepting the newly formed family member feels more like an insult than a reason to celebrate.[5]

When I learned this, I realized that these conflicting feelings were normal. I wasn't a schizo! I still occasionally feel those painful emotions. But as more time passes and our relationship grows, this conflict diminishes. When these emotions surface and your daughter wants to talk, and you feel you might blow up, say something like this: "Honey, I'd like to talk, but right now I can't handle my emotions. I'm not sure why, but I need some space. I need to deal with some of my own stuff. Give me a few hours, and then we can talk."

7. **Press the "pause" button when painful emotions tempt you to react.**

When we had almost completed our manuscript, I asked Heather to write a check to our CPA for her portion of his tax preparation fee—I asked five times. And where was the check after the fifth reminder? Nowhere. My frustration subconsciously led me down the wrong road. I began to think that her old irresponsible ways were coming back.

As my anger rose, I began to power up to vent my frustration at her. Fortunately, I began my daily jog. As I ran I prayed. That run cooled my anger, and God impressed me to change my tactic from a power play to a heart talk.

When we met later that night, I explained my hurt feelings because I felt as if she was using me. I spoke slowly, looked down a lot, and paused a lot. This defused what otherwise could have caused a rift between us. The conversation went well, she apologized, and we developed a simple plan to help her remember to do what she promises she'll do.

I learned a great lesson from this experience. Heather is still Heather—disorganized, a bit scatterbrained, and forgetful. God gave her an artistic, free-spirited personality, and he gave me a linear, engineering mind. That created conflict in her rebellious days and will continue to create conflict in these good days. But when I now push my emotional "pause" button, it helps me not react.

As Heather finishes nursing school, she has opted to live with us to save money on room and board. Her room *still* looks like a country road trash dump, although she has improved lately. (I can actually see the carpet now). She still leaves thirteen wet towels, six pairs of shoes, and past issues of *Vogue* on her bathroom floor each day. She still drops opened bags of Cheetos on the floor in the den. And she still forgets to call us when she's staying out late with friends. But Heather is Heather, she is an adult now, and I'm using my "pause" button a lot more frequently.

8. Guard against the "elder brother" syndrome.

When the prodigal son returned and his dad threw the welcome home party, the older brother became angry. The father tried to explain why they should rejoice in his brother's return. The older son refused to join the celebration.

Dad, don't become like the older brother who couldn't enjoy the good in his brother's return. Relish even the smallest improvements you see in your daughter. She will still have a long way to grow, but take joy in the progress.

I once worked in a church with a pastor who would never accept or enjoy success. We'd plan an event, execute it, and see great results. Afterwards he'd inevitably find something negative to say. He'd always preface his comments with, "Yeah, but. . . ." Don't "yeah, but" your daughter's positive changes.

9. Don't rebuff your daughter's overtures to reach out and change.

One mom, Susan, describes how she applied this point, a close cousin to the previous point. After she received a call from her wayward daughter, she shared her response.

It had been over two years since I had heard from Jill. My first reaction was, "What does she want this time?" Fortunately, I didn't say those words out loud. All she wanted was to hear my voice, to make sure I was still there. She talked for only a few minutes and said, "I'll write you a letter tomorrow, Mom," and hung up.

This letter came in the mail about a week later and told what had happened in her life over these past two years. She'd been through a lot. That phone call and the letter marked the change in our relationship. It was a small beginning, but at least it was a beginning.[6]

Dad, when your daughter reaches out to you, receive and celebrate those simple steps.

10. Relinquish them as they get older, but don't abandon.

When our daughters begin their journey home, we must let them go. Barbara Johnson, a Christian humor writer who faced deep disappointment with her children, wrote,

> Probably the very hardest thing you will ever have to do for your own recovery, and for the restoration of your relationship with your child, is to *let that child go!* Let him go and let God take over. It sounds so much easier than it really is, but it is essential to healing and restoration.[7]

God wants us to follow His ways and honor Him. But that doesn't always happen because we sin. Likewise, we want our children to do right yet they, too, will rebel. Although we must never relinquish our desire that they follow God and treat us right, we must relinquish our demand for it. John White describes relinquishment with this story.

> In days gone by market men in Covent Garden, London, used to sell caged nightingales. They captured the birds and blinded them by inserting hot needles in their eyes. Because nightingales sing in

the dark, a liquid song bubbled almost endlessly from the caged and blinded birds. Man had enslaved and blinded them to gratify his delight in their music. More than this he had enslaved them in such a manner that they could never again enjoy freedom. No one could set them free.

To relinquish our children is to set them free. The earlier we relinquish them the better. If we unthinkingly view them as objects designed for our pleasure, we may destroy their capacity for freedom just as the Covent Garden men made nightingales "unfreeable." We may also cripple ourselves. Having made our children necessary to our happiness, we can so depend on them that we grow incapable of managing without them.[8]

When our daughters return, we must relinquish our . . .

- Presumption that they must make us proud.

- Demands that they make us happy.

- Expectations that they repay us for our investment in them.

- Hunger for peaceful circumstances.

- Desire that our parenting results look respectable in other's eyes

- Yearnings that our daughters live life devoid of pain.

When we relinquish our daughters, we avoid a needless waste of our energy and the temptation to control everything about them. They need us to let them go. But in letting go, we must never abandon them.

When your daughter begins her journey back, welcome her the way this dad did.

She walks into the terminal not knowing what to expect. Not one of the thousand scenes that have played out in her mind prepares her for what she sees. There, in the concrete-walls-and-plastic-chairs bus terminal in Traverse City, Michigan, stands a group of forty brothers and sisters and great-aunts and uncles and cousins and a grandmother and great-grandmother to boot. They're all wearing goofy party hats and blowing noise-makers, and taped across the entire wall of the terminal is a computer-generated banner that reads, "Welcome home!"

Out of the crowd of well-wishers breaks her dad. She stares out through the tears quivering in her eyes like hot mercury and begins the memorized speech, "Dad, I'm sorry. I know. . . ."

He interrupts her. "Hush, child. We've got no time for that. No time for apologies. You'll be late for the party. A banquet's waiting for you at home."[9]

Relationship Lifters

- This week, ask your daughter what she fears in a renewed relationship with you. Then, you tell her what you fear. Discuss how you can overcome those fears.
- Make a list of your values that you perceive differ from hers. Ask her to evaluate that list and then talk about it. Convey to her that although you may disagree, you respect her as a person.
- Ask your daughter how you could become more of a mentor to her. Take one of her suggestions and apply it within the next five days.
- Notice every time your daughter shows a positive improvement. Tell her those improvements you see and that you're proud of her.

For Daughters

After my harrowing alcohol poisoning incident, things calmed down and my life returned to normal. One day my dad pulled me aside for a talk.

"Honey," he said, "Do you remember all those times when you told me I was being unreasonable or stupid? Well, I realize now that you were completely right.

"Therefore, I have decided to implement some changes. First of all, I understand that school is boring and time-consuming. And teachers—they can be pretty picky about things like turning in homework and showing up for tests. I think society has put too much emphasis on learning and expanding your mind. After all, it really cuts into 'hang out' time. Therefore, I have decided to make it optional. You may choose when and if you go to school. It really is such a hassle, so I won't bother you about it anymore. If you choose to sit at home eating mint-chip ice cream out of the carton and watching *Blind Date* reruns all day long, then I support you 100 percent. I love you and want to make your life as enjoyable as possible.

"Second of all, this curfew thing is rather silly. Why shouldn't you be allowed to come in at 4:30 in the morning—especially if you don't have to get up for school if you don't want to? So . . . no more curfew. Come and go as you please and when you please. And you don't have to tell me where you are or who you're with—it's okay. I trust you.

"And boys—oh, boys. It's not really any of my business who you choose to date. I'm your father—not your baby-sitter. You know, I really should be less judgmental. And tattoos, education, and age aren't really that important. And what's a little old rap sheet, or a few felonies? People change. As long as you're happy, I'm happy.

"I've also been very restrictive about your choice of dress. Why shouldn't you be able to wear what you want to? You know

185

that see-through micromini that you sneak out of the house to change into? Well, that's okay by me—you can even wear it to church if you'd like. And even though the law forbids it, you're welcome to drink alcohol. If you want, honey, I can even buy you the alcohol. I've realized that you're only young once, and you need to sow those wild oats. Just let me know when and at what time, and you can have your friends over and have a great party! Mom and I will go out of town so that we'll be out of your hair for the weekend. And I already have a repairman handy for any holes you might put in the walls or furniture you might break.

"Also, I've decided that a job is just one more thing for you to worry about. So quit it. I got you your own credit card in my name. I called the company and there is no limit, so you won't have to worry about overcharging, and it will be billed directly to me. Feel free to use it for whatever you want—skimpy clothes, music with abrasive lyrics, cigarettes—whatever your heart desires. As long as you're happy, dear.

"You no longer have to clean your room—I've hired a maid for you. Your laundry will be done, bed made, and trash picked up. Your dressers will be dusted, your shoes organized, and your CDs alphabetized. I never want you to have to lift a finger again.

"And last but not least, here are the keys to my car. I don't really need it. I like recumbent bicycles . . . I can ride that around until I can find a new car. You are my daughter, and you deserve only the best. After the alcohol incident, my eyes were opened. This wouldn't have happened if only I'd been a better parent. This means, just do whatever you want. Your happiness is much more important than my peace of mind. I need to mellow out. So thank you for teaching me this invaluable lesson. i love you, honey."

And after that talk, my dad got back on his spaceship and flew away.

If you believed this, you have either done way too many drugs or you're very gullible. This doesn't even happen in the movies!

My reentry into the family was not an easy one. We still disagreed, we still fought, and we still argued. Our relationship is definitely not (and never will be) perfect. So when things begin to improve with your dad and then start to get tough again—which they will—don't immediately assume that it's all falling apart.

Maybe you could use these few reminders to make your new relationship easier and to remind yourself not to lose it when you get into a fight.

Learn to accept and acknowledge your differences.

You can look at me and my dad and see how different we are. He's very straight-laced and conservative and enjoys classical music, boat rides, and writing books. I currently have a black "rocker mullet," I love shows and the city, and it's torture for me to do the same task for more than fifteen seconds. Our relationship works only because we make it work.

My dad, the engineer, is an organized, structured, incredibly self-disciplined planner. I am ... not. I like to do things when I feel like it, you know, spontaneously. My dad faithfully woke up every day at 6:00 a.m. on the dot to work on this book for two hours. He studied his old journals extensively, took notes, and made 215-point outlines. I, on the other hand, stared off into space, picked off my nail polish, and called everyone in my cell-phone book before I even touched the keyboard. I could type for a maximum of one hour (since my attention span lasts only for so long) while my dad painstakingly followed every detail of his outline.

We've both learned not to try to change each other, but to

accept each other for who we are. For instance, when we go on family trips (to my chagrin, when they won't let me drive separately), my dad must have control of the radio. And what does he do? With pen and legal pad in hand, he listens to teaching tapes—and takes notes. I don't know anything more frustrating than being stuck in a car for six hours with the drone of some stale man's voice ringing in your ears as you try to pass the eternity called a "family car ride" by sleeping. It drives me crazy.

But when I see the dazed look on his face when I play Ladytron or the Moving Units, I realize we're even. I've learned just to keep my mouth shut and tune out the boring man voice, and he's learned to overcome his Heather-music-induced anxiety and confusion.

My dad and I still struggle with our differing views of movies, music, styles of dress, and everything else. But we've learned to be patient with each other, talk through our problems, and work them out. We still disagree, but I've learned to keep myself under control so I won't say or do something I'll regret later.

And just remember—re-entering a relationship is starting over for the both of you. It might be a bumpy ride at first, but as time goes on, it will get easier. Don't lose hope—don't give up. It's all worth it in the end.

Don't expect a fairy tale.

You've probably discovered that building relationships is hard, hard work. The same is true with you and your dad.

Wouldn't we all love life to be like the fairy-tale story I told at the beginning of this chapter? But that's not going to happen. No relationship lacks ups and downs and good times and bad times. Dad probably won't immediately turn into the coolest man on earth, just as you probably won't immediately turn into a candidate for the Christian Daughter of the Year contest. Anticipate frustrations so that you can deal with them better. You will have setbacks. But they're natural and normal, so don't get discouraged.

My dad and I are not perfect. We still fight. We even had countless fights about writing this book, including each of us throwing stacks of incomplete drafts at each other. But we've learned to anticipate that things won't be perfect, and when a problem arises, we work it out. James 1:19 says, "Everyone should be quick to listen, slow to speak and slow to become angry." That's awesome advice. Don't expect perfection—expect someone who's human. It will be easier to begin building the new relationship if you are realistic.

And once again—the good old favorite: compromise.

I've written about this throughout the book. But I'm not just telling you this because I've run out of ideas. This has got to be the single most important aspect of a relationship. You will face tug-of-wars—he wants you to do one thing, and you want to do another, and vice versa. You must anticipate this and perhaps create a battle plan. You could work something out with your dad so you can let him know when you're getting ready to blow up. Relationships will not work without give-and-take, so prepare to bend.

A huge component of the give-and-take phenomenon is forgiveness. As the Bible says, "Be kind and compassionate to one another, forgiving each other" (Ephesians 4:32). Allow your dad to make mistakes and mess up just as you will. You must give each other room to make mistakes. So don't revert back to the old ways when he does something you're not happy with. Be prepared to forgive him—a lot. Ultimately, God gives the power to forgive and change. Even before I realized it, He was working in my heart to change me, and He still does. Without Jesus, my dad and I would have never reconciled.

Though my dad and I drive each other crazy sometimes because we are so different, we still love each other and neither of us tries to change the other. If your relationship is going to thrive, you must learn to deal with the differences between you and your dad, stay realistic, and learn to forgive.

Relationship Lifters

- Do something with your dad that you used to do together when times were better. It could be going to a movie, going for a walk, or going to the zoo. Doing those things might reawaken some of the positive feelings that you had before.
- When your dad does something cool, don't let it go unnoticed. Tell him. If you see him changing, let him know. That way, he'll know what he's doing right, and hopefully he'll keep doing it.
- Consider where God is in your life. And if He's not already included, make Him a part of it. Pick up your Bible and read a few verses a day. Pray. Find a church you like.

ℳom to ℳom

When Heather began her return, hopes of fresh starts and new beginnings ran high. But her rough edges still needed smoothing. When your daughter begins her return and you feel disappointment when her old self resurfaces, it's easy to become negative. That can sap your emotions and your motivation. Fight against that tendency.

Buckle in because you're still in for a roller-coaster ride. However, you'll find that the lows aren't as low as before. Remember that your daughter is still changing, and you both need to give each other space and some slack. This process reminds me of donkey trails that wrap around some rural mountains. Those paths—long, slow, and sometimes treacherous—are much like your daughter's return. It's easy to get caught up in the hairpin turns and falling rocks if you think about how far you need to go. Sometimes you may wonder if you're making any progress. But, if you look back, you can get a clear picture of how far you've come and the next turn won't seem so scary.

A Mother's Prayer

Father, as we seek to reconnect and move forward, give me what I need by Your Holy Spirit's power to keep encouraging, reaching out, and loving. Help me to keep Your perspective. I thank You for the progress we've made. Continue to change our whole family to reflect You fully.

ten

FOR DADS' EYES ONLY: "IS THIS ALL MY FAULT?"

The misbehaviors of our children do not necessarily
indicate that we are failures as parents. Our worth
as parents does not hinge on the choices of our children.
—Teen expert Buddy Scott[1]

My father was a wonderful dad, and he definitely made a positive impact on my parenting. But another dad actually influenced me more than the combined influence of all the fathers I've ever met. I've known this dad personally and through the eyes of others.

I'm still amazed at his fathering skills. He gave his kids everything they could have ever dreamed of, though he didn't spoil them. They came into adulthood with no emotional baggage to affect their relationships, and they lived in an incredibly beautiful home.

Unlike most of our families, these kids never experienced conflict with anyone. They lacked nothing in their relationship with their father. He was always there for them. They talked a lot, never hid things from each other, always used kind words, and never misunderstood each other.

He taught them about goodness and truth. He didn't overload them with rules, lists, and "don'ts." In fact, he only had one "don't." He wanted them to enjoy his provision for them, and they had everything they needed.

I'd classify this father as a Super Father. Unfortunately, though, his children broke his heart. Although he did everything right, they rebelled against his guidance. After that, they hid from him. When he finally confronted them, they blamed others and even him for their problems. (Has your daughter ever blamed you for her problems? Heather often blamed me.)

After their rebellion, their relationship was never the same. A great rift grew between them. Their problems even affected their kids and their kids' kids. This dad's first grandchild became a murderer. Sad, yet true.

The father you know. His name? Abba. His kids? Adam and Eve.[2]

Dads, God the Father gave Adam and Eve a perfect environment in which to live. He flawlessly provided for their needs and gave them a choice to obey or to disobey Him. Yet they chose to revolt and became the first humans to sin. He also gave our daughters, and you and me, that same free will. You and I have also rebelled against God through our sins, just as your daughters chose to rebel against you.

When guilt crouches at the door of my heart, waiting to condemn me, the creation story always encourages me. I could never parent better than my heavenly Father did (and does). We're imperfect, and although He was the perfect parent, His kids turned away. So, how can *we* possibly guarantee that our daughters won't turn away from our values? Even so, many dads struggle with guilty feelings. Though our daughters are the ones misbehaving, we carry the load of guilt and self-blame.

Some parents quickly move beyond the guilt. Most of us can't. Martha Mitchell describes guilt in this way: "It corkscrews into the depths of [our] souls, twisting and knotting, stabbing pain into every vivid memory."[2] Guilty feelings can cripple us and become an endless nightmare unless we deal with them. Dads, if you still struggle with guilt, these suggestions could help.

1. Separate true guilt from self-inflicted guilt and shame.

We live not only in a physical world, but also in an unseen spiritual world. Satan actively works against our relationships with our daughters through guilt and condemnation. Scripture describes Satan as "the accuser" (Revelation 12:10). I often felt guilty as a father even when I knew I didn't do anything wrong. That false guilt (inaccurate guilt) felt the same as the guilt I felt when I knew I was wrong (accurate guilt). Because it felt the same, it complicated my ability to sort out the true from the false. If I didn't stop my wrong thinking, Satan's accusations got the best of me, and I felt like a total failure.

We all hold some responsibility for making mistakes. I made many. Although we may blame ourselves for our daughters' behaviors, are we ultimately to blame for their wrong choices? No. Common sense should tell us that all the blame does not lie with us.

When I'd tell myself, "I'm a rotten dad . . . I'm worthless . . . Heather would be better off with another dad," I usually forced myself to challenge those shameful thoughts. Proverbs 14:15 (NAS) reminded me that "The naive believes everything, but the prudent man considers his steps." I tended to think that, in general, kids from healthy families turn out healthy and kids from troubled families turn out troubled. But common sense reminded me that's not always true.

Our family is a perfect example. Most people would describe our family as healthy and balanced. Yet Heather experienced serious problems while our other two kids

> ### *Mom's Tip*
>
> Mom, you, too, may struggle with guilt. If so, consider the suggestions in this chapter to help you deal with your pain.

didn't. I've also known emotionally healthy adults who never rebelled even though they grew up with terrible parents.

Journaling helped me keep shame and guilt from escalating to the level O'Rourke and Sauer describe: "Toxic shame is the kind that leaves you believing that you are hopelessly defective and undeserving of acceptance. Healthy shame serves the purpose of self-correction and character growth."[4] Try journaling to help you sort out your feelings.

If journaling doesn't appeal to you, take out a piece of paper and draw a line down the center. At the very top write, "What do I feel guilty about?" Then, over the left column write, "What's true?" and over the right column write, "What's false?" Take time alone with God and write down whatever comes to mind in both categories. Don't overanalyze, though. God will bring to mind what needs to go on your list. After you finish your list, go down your "What's false?" column and strike through each item. As you do, repeat Romans 8:1 aloud, "Therefore, there is now no condemnation for those who are in Christ Jesus." Hang on to your list and go to this next suggestion.

2. Admit your actual failures. Just don't believe *you* are a failure.

Norm Wright captured the truth about our imperfect fathering when he wrote,

> You have failed in the past. So have I.
> You are failing now in some way. So am I.
> You will fail in the future. So will I.
> You were not perfect in the past. Neither was I.
> You are not perfect now. Neither am I.
> You will not be perfect in the future. Neither will I.[5]

Let's face it. We all blow it sometimes with our daughters. I wish I had given Heather more attention when our youngest daughter faced three brain surgeries. I wish I had stopped obsessing with the start of a new church so I could have spent more time with her. I wish I'd been less controlling. You probably have your wish list, as did another father I know. He once angrily grabbed his daughter's homework paper and crumpled it up because he thought she wasn't studying enough. As he shared this with me, tears flowed down his cheeks as he said, "I still have that crumpled paper in my drawer."

Dads, if you still cling to your crumpled failures to remind you of your guilt, it's time to throw them away! The Message translation boldly states, "Generous in love—God, give grace! Huge in mercy—wipe out my bad record. Scrub away my guilt, soak out my sins in your laundry" (Psalm 51:1–2).

Continue the list you began in the previous step. Now go down your list of "What's true?" and admit your failures to God. As you admit them and ask God's cleansing, use a red pen to obliterate each failure. Thank Him for forgiving you. Remind yourself that God will never again bring these up against you. Psalm 103:12 states, "How far has the LORD taken our sins from us? Farther than the distance from east to west!" Realize, though, that your shameful feelings may not disappear overnight. You may need to repeat this process.

To complete this exercise, you must ask your daughter to forgive you. At an appropriate time, admit your failures to her. Don't wait for her to admit her guilt. Don't defend, make excuses, or blame. Just say, "Honey, I was wrong when I— [fill in the blank]. Please forgive me."

Let her respond in the way she chooses. She may find it difficult to receive your confession. She may blow you off or say, "No big deal." Her response is not the issue; your confession is the issue. Once you do this, the process doesn't end. You'll still blow up sometimes, say something you shouldn't, or give her the cold shoulder. When that happens, quickly admit your guilt to her and again ask for forgiveness. When you unjustly offend her, don't let a lot of time pass before you ask her to forgive you.

> ### Mom's Tip
>
> Mom, if, mentally and verbally, your husband beats himself with "if only," become his greatest encourager. Remind him that although God perfectly parented Adam and Eve, they still rebelled.

I still mess up and must ask all my kids to forgive me. Not only does my confession keep me emotionally healthy, but it softens Heather's heart as well. One November I realized I had hurt her, so I called to ask her to forgive me. After she heard my genuine confession, she asked me to pray for her. That was a big deal to me because she seldom asked for prayer during those tough years.

After you admit your own failures, eliminate "if only" from your vocabulary once and for all. If I were to make a list of all the things of things I wish I could do over, I'd write a book. (I did. You're reading it.)

I've shared several of my failures. If I could take them back, I would. But I can't. Even if I could, there's no guarantee that Heather would have made wise choices. Early in the process I decided I'd quit berating myself with *If only I'd done this or that differently, then we wouldn't have faced those problems with Heather.* Instead, I owned my own guilt, and not hers.

Dads, if you mentally hammer yourself with "if only," ask God to make you aware of those negative thoughts. Share your struggle with a close male friend and make yourself accountable to him. Give him permission to ask you how you're doing.

Remember the quote at the beginning of this chapter from Buddy Scott: "Our worth as parents does not hinge on the choices of our children."

3. Guard yourself from those who make you feel guilty.

Parents without rebellious teens can seldom identify with the struggle we face. Their misguided comments or outright accusations often add to our pain. Their words become "like pouring vinegar in an open cut" (Proverbs 25:20 CEV).

One mom with a struggling teen shared this: "Far worse than blaming myself was my mother pointing the finger at me. She came right out and said, 'What can you expect when you made mistakes yourself?' It was as though she were saying, 'You deserve this.'"[6]

Dads, when you become the brunt of others' intentional or unintentional accusations, don't react with your own caustic words. It will only deepen your guilt. When their words bring guilty feelings, remind yourself that your daughter chose her path. Seek to minimize careless comments of old friends by choosing new friends wisely. You do not bear the guilt of the consequences of her choices. Let the words of the prophet Ezekiel encourage you: "The child does not share the guilt of the parent, nor the parent the guilt of the child" (18:20 MSG).

Ruth Graham, wife of Billy Graham, wrote a tender book after dealing with her own prodigal, Franklin. She included a poem that describes a common experience we feel with our prodigals.

THEY FELT GOOD EYES UPON THEM

They felt good eyes upon them
and shrank within—undone;
good parents had good children
and they—a wandering one.

The good folk never meant
to act smug or condemn,
but having prodigals,
just "wasn't done" with them.

Remind them gently, Lord,
how you have trouble with your children,
too.[7]

4. Make sure that you've let Jesus wipe your guilt away.

Parenting typical daughters challenges us enough. But parenting difficult daughters takes resources beyond our abilities. Although our heads can tell us that peer pressure, genetic predisposition, and temptations of society may have all contributed to our daughters' rebellion. Yet our hearts often disagree because emotion often trumps logic. Cognitively we know that we don't bear all the guilt. We, therefore, can embrace the suggestions outlined.

A personal relationship with Christ will help your heart heal from the pangs of guilt. When we admit our sins to Him and accept His payment on the cross for those sins, He completely forgives us and wipes away our guilt. When we experience and live in forgiveness, guilt won't strangle us.

Dads, examine your relationship with Jesus. If you've not yet come to faith in Him, consider it. If you'd like to pursue that relationship with Him, begin by reading the book of John in the Bible and find a good nearby church.

When Christ comes into your life, He will lift the black cloud of guilt. The apostle Paul wrote, "With the arrival of Jesus, the Messiah, that fateful dilemma is resolved. Those who enter into Christ's being-here-for-us no longer have to live under a continuous, low-lying black cloud" (Romans 8:1 MSG).

When we experience a true relationship with Jesus and freedom from guilt, we can divert our energies into healthy spiritual practices. We don't need to beat ourselves up with neurotic guilt nor shame ourselves for our inadequacies. Rather, we should give that energy to praying that our daughters will see truth and act upon it.

Relationship Lifters

- This week, take some time to work through your guilt—both accurate and inaacurate.
- Within a week after that, admit your failures to your daughter and ask her to forgive you.
- Evaluate your current friends. If some induce guilt, let them know how they make you feel. They may not even be aware of it. Deepen your relationships with those who don't induce guilt. Perhaps you'll want to add friends who know from experience what you're going through.

Mom to Mom

I wasn't prepared for what the teenage years brought. I came into the job with faulty reasoning. I poured my energy into Heather to teach, train, and mold her character to reflect Christ's. I assumed that once we weathered the preteen hormonal shifts with no major snags, then the mold was set. Perhaps she'd need a periodic tweak as she matured, but nothing more. So I felt devastated when our Christian-character-award daughter flushed those values down the toilet and become our worst nightmare.

When that happened, guilt, humiliation, and shame enveloped me. When the shock lessened, I asked, "What did I do wrong?" I later discovered that most parents in similar situations feel the same way. Although we do our best to parent our children, we can't control many of their choices. It doesn't help them or us when we wallow in guilt. I reminded myself that even God the Father parents rebellious children. We have all rebelled. He knows the pain we bring Him, and therefore He will meet us in our pain.

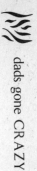
A Mother's Prayer

Lord, I bring You all my guilt,
shame, and brokenness.
Embrace me with Your tender mercies.
Thank You that You love and accept me
in spite of the bad choices
my daughter makes.

eleven

FOR DAUGHTERS' EYES ONLY: THE HIGH PRICE OF "FREE" SEX

*I don't know when the boys / began to walk away
with parts of myself / in their sticky hands; / when loving /
became a process of subtraction . . .*
—Melissa Stein[1]

The icy snowflakes nipped at my face, and the freezing air mingled with the hot tears that flowed freely down my cheeks.

I continued to plunge the hand shovel into the frozen ground, intent on deepening the hole by the tiny sapling. I paused and surveyed my surroundings. The snow coated the tall pines and swirled around us as if we were trapped inside a giant snow globe. The gray sky gave the perfect backdrop for what we had to do that day. I looked at my best friend. She didn't look up; she just kept digging. Our hands were red and numb from the snow as we finished our "project." That was the day it would finally be "settled." This was her way of closure.

But there was never a way to undo the past, there was no real forgetting.

Every day we choose. We make simple choices—what to eat, what to wear, what calls to return. We make the more difficult choices—Do I sneak out tonight? Do I smoke this? Do I skip school today? And sometimes we make the choices that will affect us indefinitely . . . some of which leave scars forever.

205

The unalterable, undoable life-changing decision had already been made; this was only an attempt to find some kind of peace. Sadly, it could never truly cover the gaping wound left by its consequences.

My friend and I stood and somberly faced each other. Our teary, red-rimmed eyes locked. I read a few verses from my worn Bible. The mixture of my continuing tears and the wet snow hitting the pages made the words difficult to read. Weeping, I struggled to eke out the last words of the passage. We gathered over our hole, held each other's hands for support, and said a soft prayer.

Then we knelt in the snow and gathered the things scattered around us. She had brought a few pictures that were dear to her, a tiny wooden music box she'd had since she was a little girl, a hand-written song on a crumpled piece of notebook paper, pink ribbons, buttons, dried leaves, and other mementos she valued. I'd gathered together what I could find that was right for the occasion: a tiny stuffed dog, a letter I had written, a picture, flowers. We placed our things in the tiny hole. We gathered the frozen bits of dirt and snow and slowly began to fill it. The ice tumbled onto the dog's fur, smeared the ink on the letters, and dirtied the pictures. I set a wild-flower on the white and brown mound that now lay below the small sapling. I looked at her, and we once again exchanged looks that words cannot describe. I held her hand as we trudged away.

The realization of it hit me like a semi-truck. That day was the direct result of a choice. Sadly, and often realized too late, conse-quences affect more than us. They color our worlds, affect our lives, and determine the kinds of people we are now, and some-times the kind of people we're going to be.

There's more to a consequence than just the consequence—there are everlasting reminders of what we choose to do. The effects of what we choose to do reverberate in our lives for years to come.

You see, we weren't just digging holes and burying things

meaningful to us. That was a funeral for a little girl named Rain. Rain never had the chance to run, to play, to laugh, to smile; she never even had the chance to be born.

Rain was a casualty of a choice that someone made, a life that was affected irreparably by that choice. Rain was a victim of abortion.

That day, I felt the weight of consequence. I felt the weight of a burden that must be carried to the grave. I felt the heartbreak of a life that never had the chance to live. I felt the permanence of choices that we make, consequences that follow, and how easy it is to make a mistake that will forever change our lives.

For some reason, God chose to spare me from ever becoming pregnant. I'm glad I was never faced with that decision. My best friend got pregnant and panicked. In an act of desperation, she tried to cover up her mistake, just as most of us do.

Rain was the result of a choice: sex. Don't fool yourself: sex is not free. You can never get back the pieces of yourself that you've given away ... and you will have to deal with the consequences of your actions.

After I'd had sex with my latest "boyfriend," I felt as if I'd taken pieces of my own heart and handed them out to a guy who cared nothing for me past having a "good time." I can never get those pieces back. Yes, God has restored me. He has forgiven me and given me peace about the things I've done. But, just as a shattered vase glued back together is never quite the same, after giving yourself to someone in such a physical, spiritual, and emotional way, there's no going back.

Sex is not free. You may not end up with a tiny life hanging in the balance, but consider the obvious risks, such as sexually transmitted diseases (some of which don't have any symptoms so you won't know if you have them or if you're spreading them); feeling as if the only thing you're worth is sex; feeling objectified, dirty, used.

It's not worth it. It's just not. Sex is not free.

Sometimes I still feel that pieces of me lie scattered all over, held in the pockets of men I don't even talk to. They may never know that they carry around a part of me; they've probably never even given it that much thought. But they do ... and I know.

Don't do it. I know you've heard the after-school specials, the pastors, the youth group speakers, moms, dads, counselors, whoever, tell you, "Don't have sex. It's bad. Blah blah blah."

You know what? They know something that you haven't realized yet. You're worth more than some guy who's not willing to love you for better or worse, until death do you part. You're priceless, you're unique, you're beautiful. You are you and only you—there is no one else like you.

The Bible says, "For you created my inmost being; you knit me together in my mother's womb. I praise you because I am fearfully and wonderfully made; your works are wonderful, I know that full well" (Psalm 139:13–14). Don't give the gift of yourself away to anyone short of the man who will love you for the rest of your life.

Whenever I hear the soft pitter-patter of raindrops against my window, I remember Rain. I go back to that cold day and the little girl we memorialized with our tiny funeral. All I have now is the legacy of a child gone forever, and the shared pain of a best friend. Sex is not free. Don't fool yourself. Life-changing consequences result from a few minutes of lust.

And when you hear that familiar pitter-patter against a windowpane, remember the little girl who never had a breath, a chance, a life ... all because of the consequence of a choice gone wrong.

Be wise. Don't let the choices of today impact you forever. I bet there's one little girl who wishes she could tell you that herself.

twelve

FINAL WORDS

What I will remember is a man that changed my life. He was
always there for me when I needed him. He had a way
of putting everything into perspective, and I believe that his deter-
mination and perseverance came from his relationship with the
Lord. He played an important role in pointing me to God.
—Michael Reagan, in remarks at a memorial
service for his father, Ronald Reagan[1]

For Dads

"Sit down, Josh!" I screamed over the sound of the menacing waves. "We're about to sink!"

That summer's family vacation had taken an interesting turn. I almost drowned, along with my son and his friend. Every year we stayed a week at the beach in a sixth-floor condo that overlooked the Atlantic. That year I brought our boat, a twenty-two-foot, ivory-white, fiberglass deckboat with foam-green trim and a navy-blue bimini top. I had owned the boat less than a year and had learned to operate it on Saturday trips to our local lake. Although the ocean would give me a new boating challenge, I felt confident that my skills would help me navigate the Atlantic.

Early one morning, Josh, his friend, and I set out to catch sand sharks. As the two-hundred-horsepower outboard powered us from the bay, past the jetties and into the ocean, we were excited about the trip. We cruised out almost two miles, hooked a few two-foot sharks, and headed back in at noon. As we approached the jetties that protected the bay, I noticed swirling water a few hundred yards offshore. My curiosity prompted me to idle over to find out whether baitfish caused the swirls, as that would mean catchable fish below them.

Much to my surprise, baitfish did not cause the swirls. Rather, the confluence of the bay and the ocean at a tide change created a mini-whirlpool that began to suck us into its vortex. Six-foot waves began to crash over us as water poured into the boat from all sides. Within seconds the water rose to my knees, our white cooler floated past me down the center of the boat, and we listed dangerously toward the stern. Josh and his friend thought our predicament funny until I screamed that we were about to sink. They immediately flung themselves to the benches and clung to the stainless steel railings with white-knuckle grips.

Fortunately, the water hadn't yet killed the batteries so the bilge pump still worked. As it labored to pump out the briny water, I hit the gas and accelerated out of the mini-storm. We almost lost the boat and could have lost our lives as well. That experience gave me a new appreciation for the Coast Guard's requirement for all boats: PFDs, short for *personal flotation devices,* commonly called "life preservers." I knew that if we had sunk, we'd have had a chance to ride out the "storm" only if we hung on to our life preservers long enough for someone to rescue us.

Navigating Heather through the teenage years almost drowned me in a vortex of pain, anger, and disappointment. At times I felt I could barely gasp for air between each new conflict. Were it not for the relational "life preservers" we've shared in this book, my relationship with Heather could not have weathered those five tumultuous years. But it did. Our relationship is stronger than ever.

Dads, if you feel pulled into a similar vortex by your daughters, grab onto a few of these life preservers. They won't necessarily take

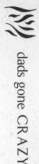
you out of the vortex, but with God's help they can help you hang on until the storm passes. Sometimes our daughters can't learn life's important lessons without making foolish choices that drive us crazy.

As John White says, "All is not lost when our children make foolish choices. It will be painful for us to watch them eat hogs' food, but there is hope that when that happens they will learn from experience what they never could have learned from precept."[2]

In each chapter I've described a relational life preserver and suggested practical ways to implement it. Here they are, for one last review.

1. Don't panic at the first warning signs.
2. Resist turning words into weapons.
3. Make the tough calls.
4. Stoke the relationship fire to keep it alive.
5. Reconnect through gifts from the heart.
6. Laugh between the tears.
7. Choose your battles—and lose some on purpose.
8. Cling to hope when you're at the bottom.
9. Soften the reentry.

Dads, at times you may feel that your daughters will never change. I can't guarantee that they will even if you use these principles. I can guarantee that as God empowers you to apply them, you can make it through these tough times. And, as time passes, odds are in your favor that the storm will pass. Perhaps your story will turn out like one written over a hundred years ago.

In the late 1800s a minister named John Watson became a well-known fiction writer. Using the pen name Ian Maclaren, he wrote a book of stories about a fictional village called Drumtochty. In one story he described the pain a father, Lachlan Campbell, felt when his daughter, Flora, left his home and his Christian values.[3]

Lachlan, an elder of the church, stood at one elders' meeting and agonizingly explained what had happened to Flora. Grieved, he said that Flora has "left home and gone into the far country." With trembling hands he read a final letter she left before she went to London. In emotion-laden words she wrote, "I will never see you again, in this world or the next. . . ." The father, a harsh man, asked the elders to remove her name from the church rolls. With compassion the other elders responded, "With the Lord there is mercy, and with Him is plenteous redemption. . . . You must not think she is gone forever."

The father, however, closed his heart to his daughter, slammed the door shut. As an act of finality he told the pastor that though they would not remove her name from the church's book, "I have blotted out her name from my Bible, where her mother's name is written and mine . . . I have no daughter." The pastor shook his hand in silence, they parted, and Lachlan turned to walk back to his cottage. He watched until the old man's figure disappeared into the cold moonlight.

Later Lachlan even remarked to a friend, Marget, who was concerned about his response, "She isn't anything to me this day . . . she has been a black shame to her name."

Marget's heart broke, and she responded, "Woe is me if our Father had blotted out our names from the Book o' Life when we left His house. But he sent His Son to seek us, an' a weary road He came. I tell you, a man would not leave a sheep to perish as you have cast off your own child."

Her words began to change Lachlan's heart. When Marget sensed that change, she wrote a letter to Flora to urge her to return. The letter assured her that her father would receive her back. Marget mailed the letter and waited to see what would happen.

Lachlan knew that if Flora came back home, she would come at night. So he took a lamp used only for show and cleaned and trimmed it. He set it on a stand next to the window so that every night its light shone down the steep path ascending to their home. Beside it lay the Bible where her dad had blotted out Flora's name.

Flora received the letter and decided to return. She began her trip on a train and then stayed a night with a friend before she walked home. As she approached the cottage, her heart jumped because she saw light blaze from the kitchen window. For a moment she thought Lachlan might be sick. However, when she suddenly realized the truth, her heart quickly filled with joy, and she ran the rest of the way because she knew the light was her welcome home.

As the dogs barked when she stepped on the porch, her father began to unlatch the door, saying, "Flora, Flora" over and over again. With speech prepared, the only word she could get out was "Father" because Lachlan, who had never even kissed her as a child, embraced her and poured out his love on her. Later, Flora told Marget that her father, who spoke Gaelic, used over fifty words for "darling" as he showered her with kisses.

As a final step to repair the relationship, Lachlan brought the Bible to her to show her the family register where he had marked out her name. With sorrow he asked for her forgiveness. She then took a pen and wrote,

FLORA CAMPBELL,
Missed April 1873.
Found September 1873.[3]

Although Heather's return didn't happen as dramatically as Flora's, she did eventually come back. I can only imagine the regret we'd now feel had we not persisted in our love long enough to see her change.

Dads (and moms), your daughters may be far from your hearts, your faith, and your families. If so, stand fast. Don't give up. Trust God. Pay the price, whether in time, tears, or money to give your daughters every chance to return. Believe that the day will come when you can celebrate that your daughters are "found." Lachlan did. So did the father of the prodigal son. We did. We paid a great price.

It was worth it.

≋

For Daughters

I have agonized over these finals words for days now. I've started over at least twenty times. I keep praying, "God, what am I supposed to say to these girls? What do they need to hear?" And still, I don't really know. Maybe that is what you need to hear: that I don't know. Sure, I may be a different person from the one I was several years ago, but I don't have everything figured out. I'm not perfect, and neither is my world. I still laugh, and I still cry. Sometimes I'm happy, and sometimes I'm lonely. I get excited about things. And sometimes I just want to give up on all of it. I still haven't figured out how to do this thing called "life."

But the one thing that keeps me going is this: God is sovereign. He's in control of every little thing in every little way. I never know what's going to happen with my life—I never would have guessed that I'd write a book about my mistakes and my life beyond them. But what I do know is that God is in control, and I've got to trust Him. This book is proof of the fact that when I take my eyes off of God, even for a second, just like Peter, I cease to walk on water and begin to sink into the depths of the sea. When I stop trusting Him, I am hopelessly lost. Everything good or right that I have ever done has been only because of His grace. He has been teaching me this every day, in so many ways, over and over again.

I hope you know by now that I'm not going to tell you something that I don't truly believe—something I say only because it sounds good, or because it's what I'm "supposed" to say. I'm going to tell you what's on my heart. So please hear me: don't shut God out. I've talked about dads this whole time, but now I'm talking about your heavenly Dad. Pray, if even for a moment. Read the Bible, if it's even just one verse. I promise you: if you take that one tiny step, He will meet you where you are.

As I was trying to write this chapter, I e-mailed one of my dearest friends, and true to his fix-it nature, he responded with one of the most beautiful messages I've ever read. In it, he talks about David's words in Psalm 139—look it up!— and he states perfectly what I had struggled for so long to say. Here it is:

> The Author and Perfecter of the universe knows your name, knows the number of hairs on your head, knows your every breath. More than that, He loves you like a groom loves a bride, like a parent loves a child. His love for you has traveled time and space. Even more, His love has traveled to the depths of the grave, through the darkest corners of sin for you. This is the greatest mystery and the greatest exercise of His sovereignty.

He continues this way:

> Every wreck I've caused in my life, every painful turn my life has taken is part of the plan He ordained for me from the beginning of time. While He was creating the earth I walk on and the stars I stand in awe of, He paused to smile upon my clumsy feet.

He ends with these final words:

> It's hard to accept grace from the supreme power of the universe, but that's exactly what He wants. He's viewing your life like a movie He's seen before—He wants you to trust that His ending, and the path to it, are sufficient. As our souls moan in the

trials of life, He leans down to whisper, "Rest in me, little David, and dry all your tears. You can lay down your armor and have no fear. 'Cause I'm always here when you're tired of running, and I'm all the strength that you need."[4]

Wherever you are right now, I hope that you will let God catch you where you've fallen and astound you with His boundless, overwhelming love. He is always, always waiting.

ENDNOTES

CHAPTER 1—THE FIRST TATTOO

1. Dr. Kevin Lehman, *Adolescence Isn't Terminal* (Wheaton, Ill.: Tyndale House, 2002), 68.
2. Chap and Dee Clark, *Daughters and Dads* (Colorado Springs, Colo.: NavPress, 1998), 106–107.
3. Scott Larson, *When Teens Stray: Parenting for the Long Haul* (Ann Arbor, Mich.: Servant, 2002), 33–34. Used by permission.
4. H. Norman Wright, *Loving a Prodigal* (Colorado Springs, Colo.: Chariot Victor, 1999), 135.
5. David and Claudia Arp, *Suddenly They're 13: A Parent's Survival Guide for the Adolescent Years* (Grand Rapids, Mich.: Zondervan, 1999), 89.
6. John White, *Parents in Pain* (Downers Grove, Ill.: InterVarsity, 1979), 62.
7. Robert J. Morgan, *Moments for Families with Prodigals* (Colorado Springs, Colo.: NavPress, 2003), 15.
8. Miles McPherson, *Parenting the Wild Child* (Minneapolis, Minn.: Bethany House, 2000), 12.
9. McPherson, *Wild Child,* 27.

Endnotes

CHAPTER 2—VERBAL VENOM

1. John White, *Parents in Pain* (Downers Grove, Il.: InterVarsity Press, 1979), 83.
2. White, *Pain,* 82.
3. Scott Larson, *When Teens Stray: Parenting for the Long Haul* (Ann Arbor, Mich.: Servant, 2002), 101–102. Used by permission.
4. Norm Wright, *Always Daddy's Girl* (Ventura, Calif.: Regal, 1998), 227. Used by permission.
5. Dave and Claudia Arp, *Suddenly They're 13: A Parent's Survival Guide for the Adolescent Years* (Grand Rapids, Mich.: Zondervan), 85. Used by permission of the Zondervan Corporation.
6. Phil Waldrep, *Parenting Prodigals* (Friendswood, Tex.: Baxter, 2001), 197.

CHAPTER 3—THE WAVE GOODBYE

1. H. Norman Wright, *Loving a Prodigal* (Colorado Springs, Colo.: Chariot Victor, 1999), 19.
2. One nonprofit Web site, http://www.wilderness-programs.org, is a good place to start. It lists and rates scores of programs. A Web search will also show companies that exist to help parents evaluate which one would best suit their teen.
3. Buddy Scott, *Relief for Hurting Parents: How to Fight for the Lives of Teenagers* (Lake Jackson, Tex.: Allon reprint ed. 1994), 224.

CHAPTER 4—WHEN LOVE LANGUISHED

1. John White, *Parents in Pain* (Downers Grove, Ill.: InterVarsity, 1979), 63.
2. Buddy Scott, *Relief for Hurting Parents: How to Fight for the Lives of Teenagers* (Lake Jackson, Tex.: Allon, reprint ed., 1994), 117.
3. Max Lucado, *The Applause of Heaven* (Nashville, Tenn.: W Publishing Group, 1990), 113–114.
4. Brendan O'Rourke and DeEtte Sauer, *The Hope of a Homecoming* (Colorado Springs, Colo.: NavPress, 2003), adapted from 77–79. Used by permission of NavPress. All rights reserved.
5. O'Rourke and Sauer, *Homecoming,* 75.
6. John Eldredge, *Waking the Dead* (Nashville, Tenn.: Thomas Nelson, 2003), p. 43.

7. Eldredge, *Waking,* 42.
8. "It's the Most Wonderful Time of the Year." © 1963 by Eddie Pola and George Wyle. Permission granted by Barnaby Music Corp.
9. Eldredge, *Waking,* 42.

CHAPTER 5—THE HALLMARK MOMENTS
1. Phil Waldrep, *Parenting Prodigals* (Friendswood, Tex.: Baxter, 2001), 136–137.
2. S. Rutherford McDill, Jr., *Parenting the Prodigal* (Waterloo, Ont.: Herald, 1996), 49.
3. Waldrep, *Prodigals,* 137–138.
4. Robert Veninga, *A Gift of Hope* (New York: Ballantine Books, 1985), 150.

CHAPTER 6—I SCREWED SHUT HER WINDOWS AND SHE STILL ESCAPED
1. From Robert Wolgemuth, *She Calls Me Daddy* (Colorado Springs, Colo.: Focus on the Family/Tyndale House, 1996), 121. All rights reserved. International copyright secured. Used by permission.
2. Cal Samra, *The Joyful Christ: The Healing Power of Humor* (San Francisco: HarperSanFrancisco, 1986), 56. Samra also is editor of *The Joyful Noiseletter* (800-877-2757, www.joyfulnoiseletter.com).
3. Samra, *Joyful Christ,* 16.
4. Chap and Dee Clark, *Daughters and Dads* (Colorado Springs, Colo.: NavPress, 1998), 160.
5. Samra, *Joyful Christ,* 203.
6. S. Rutherford McDill, Jr., *Parenting the Prodigal* (Waterloo, Ont.: Baxter, 1996), 75.
7. Samra, *Joyful Christ,* 19.
8. H. Norm Wright, *Always Daddy's Girl: Understanding Your Father's Impact on Who You Are* (Ventura, Calif.: Regal, 2001), 143. Used by permission.
9. Dallas Willard, *The Divine Conspiracy* (San Francisco: HarperSanFrancisco, 1998), 238.

Endnotes

CHAPTER 7—THE WAR ZONE

1. David and Claudia Arp, *Suddenly They're 13: A Parent's Survival Guide for the Adolescent Years* (Grand Rapids, Mich.: Zondervan, 1999), 116. Used by permission of the Zondervan Corporation.
2. Arp, *Suddenly,* 157.
3. Bruce Narramore, "Teenage Negativism: How Much is Normal?" *Psychology for Living* (September-October 2000), 9.
4. Kevin Lehman, *Adolescence Isn't Terminal* (Wheaton, Ill.: Tyndale, 2002), 95.
5. Lehman, *Terminal,* 96.
6. Scott Larson, *When Teens Stray: Parenting for the Long Haul* (Ann Arbor, Mich.: Servant, 2002), 130–132. Used by permission.

CHAPTER 8—HOPELESS IN THE ER

1. John White, *Parents in Pain* (Downers Grove, Ill.: InterVarsity, 1979), 220.
2. Max Lucado, *No Wonder They Call Him the Savior* (Portland, Ore.: Multnomah, 1986), 106.
3. S. Rutherford McDill, Jr., *Parenting the Prodigal* (Waterloo, Ont.: Baxter, 1996), 114.
4. Quin Sherrer and Ruthanne Garlock, *Praying Prodigals Home* (Ventura, Calif.: Regal, 2000), 29–30.
5. Larry Crabb, *Connecting* (Nashville, Tenn.: Word, 1997), 115.
6. Ron Mehl, *God Works the Night Shift* (Sisters, Ore.: Multnomah, 1994), 130.
7. Brendan O'Rourke, Ph.D., and DeEtte Sauer, *The Hope of a Homecoming* (Colorado Springs, Colo.: NavPress, 2003), 95. Used by permission of NavPress. All rights reserved.
8. O'Rourke and Sauer, *Homecoming,* 139.
9. Taken from anonymous emails listed on the Web site http://www.Imissmydad.com. After extensive research, we were unable to locate the authors. If the writers of the e-mails are located, we will be happy to give appropriate credit.

CHAPTER 9—THE PRODIGAL RETURNS

1. Quin Sherrer and Ruthanne Garlock, *Praying Prodigals Home* (Ventura, Calif.: Regal, 2000), 199. Used by permission.
2. Woodrow Kroll, *Surviving the Prodigals in Your Life* (Lincoln, Neb.: Back to the Bible Publishing, 2001), 141.

3. Gary and Dr. Greg Smalley, *Bound by Honor* (Wheaton, Ill.: Tyndale, 1980), 198.
4. Chap and Dee Clark, *Daughters and Dads* (Colorado Springs, Colo.: NavPress, 1998), 99.
5. Brendan O' Rourke, Ph.D., and DeEtte Sauer, *The Hope of a Homecoming* (Colorado Springs, Colo.: NavPress, 2003), 172.
6. Marcia Mitchell, *Surviving the Prodigal Years* (Lynnwood, Wash.: Emerald Books, 1995), 153.
7. Barbara Johnson, *Fresh Elastic for Stretched-Out Moms* (Grand Rapids, Mich.: Revell, 1986), 164.
8. John White, *Parents in Pain* (Downers Grove, Ill.: InterVarsity, 1979), 164.
9. Philip Yancey, *What's So Amazing about Grace?* (Grand Rapids, Mich.: Zondervan, 1997), 51.

CHAPTER 10—FOR DADS' EYES ONLY

1. Buddy Scott, *Relief for Hurting Parents: How to Fight for the Lives of Teenagers* (Lake Jackson, Tex.: Allon, reprint ed., 1994), 15.
2. Ibid., p. 11.
3. Marcia Mitchell, *Surviving the Prodigal Years* (Lynnwood, Wash.: Emerald, 1995), 76.
4. Brendan O'Rourke, Ph.D. and DeEtte Sauer, *The Hope of a Homecoming* (Colorado Springs, Colo.: NavPress, 2003), 59–60. Used by permission. All rights reserved.
5. H. Norman Wright, *Loving a Prodigal* (Colorado Springs, Colo.: Chariot Victor, 1999), 47.
6. Mitchell, *Surviving*, 77.
7. Ruth Bell Graham, *Prodigals (and Those Who Love Them)* (Grand Rapids, Mich.: Baker, 1999), 144.

FOR DAUGHTERS' EYES ONLY

1. Melissa Stein, *Love Letter,* reprinted by permission of the author.

FINAL WORDS

1. Quoted from public documents.
2. John White, *Parents in Pain* (Downers Grove, Ill.: InterVarsity, 1979), 200.
3. Ian Maclaren, *Beside the Bonnie Brier Bush* (Dodd, Mead and Company, 1985), adapted from public domain material.
4. "Lullaby" lyrics by Pedro the Lion. Used by permission.

For more information or to arrange speaking engagements for Charles or Heather, please visit our website at

www.wilddaughters.com